PRAISE FOR *BUIL*
DIGITAL CULTURE

C000254341

'Thorough and methodically researched, supported by relevant examples from recognized industry names, this book provides practical tips and suggestions that will help marketers dealing day to day with multiple digital challenges.'
Sholto Douglas-Home, Chief Marketing Officer, Hays plc

'Full of sharp insight and practical advice on how to think, build and navigate "digital" in the totally transparent world of tomorrow.'
Markus Kramer, Partner, Brand Affairs AG (and former CMO, Aston Martin Lagonda)

'A genuinely inspiring, thought-provoking and motivational read wherever you are in your organization and at whatever stage of your digital maturity.'
Neil Costello, Head of Marketing, Atom Bank

'Packed full of actionable ideas, relevant case studies and insight-driven thought-starters.'
Vicki Davis, Head of Film Marketing, Universal Pictures Home Entertainment

'A very well researched and written book that is an essential aid to help you navigate through the potentially vexatious digital world.'
Nick Hughes, Director of Marketing and Communications, SEGRO plc

'A great starter pack for anyone who wants to be serious about diving into the digital age and driving change. It's surely not an easy task and this book gives a lot of great advice about where to start and what to focus on.'
Thierry Campet, Global Head of Marketing and Communications, UBS Wealth Management

'Very few titles offer peer-driven help. This does. Full of depth, it offers a terrific blend of pragmatism, inspiration and reassurance to those (like myself) involved in business transformation projects. A book to read and then reference as each challenge arises.'
Duncan Daines, Chief Marketing Officer, Gama Aviation plc

'Shows real experience of the challenges with change and transformation. The advice and case studies give brilliant insight into how to reality check your own organization and your own vision! There is courage in these pages – challenging and well-used terms and methodologies, but addressed in a helpful and practical way. A book to share.'
Eda Colbert, Head of Brand and Marketing, British Council

'A great combination of practical tips, real-life examples and honest advice on how, or how not, to deliver change through digital transformation.'
Anne Godfrey, Chief Executive, CIEH

'The breakneck speed of today's digital environment is challenging for all marketers to keep up with. This book will help marketers from start-ups to large businesses to take a firmer grip of this digital environment, and better use its capabilities to deliver greater levels of traffic, revenue and profit.'
Simon Daggett, Global Head of Marketing, DHL Global Forwarding

'Finally, digital has been distilled and debunked! Not surprisingly, in *Building Digital Culture*, Thomas Brown's strategic, wood-for-the-trees perspective combines brilliantly with Daniel Rowles' depth and breadth on all things digital, resulting in a no-nonsense, actionable guide to digital capability building, regardless of where you are on the journey.'
Cesar Lastra, Founding Director, Bash and Build

Building Digital Culture

A practical guide to successful digital transformation

Daniel Rowles
Thomas Brown

KoganPage

First published in Great Britain and the United States in 2017 by Kogan Page Limited

2nd Floor, 45 Gee Street	c/o Martin P Hill Consulting	4737/23 Ansari Road
London EC1V 3RS	122 W 27th St, 10th Floor	Daryaganj
United Kingdom	New York NY 10001	New Delhi 110002
www.koganpage.com	USA	India

© Daniel Rowles and Thomas Brown, 2017

The right of Daniel Rowles and Thomas Brown to be identified as the authors of this work has been asserted by them in accordance with the Copyright, Designs and Patents Act 1988.

ISBN   978 0 7494 7965 7
E-ISBN   978 0 7494 7966 4

British Library Cataloguing-in-Publication Data

A CIP record for this book is available from the British Library.

Library of Congress Cataloging-in-Publication Data

Names: Rowles, Daniel, author. | Brown, Thomas, 1982- author.
Title: Building digital culture : a practical guide to successful digital
    transformation / Daniel Rowles and Thomas Brown.
Description: London ; New York : Kogan Page, 2017. | Includes bibliographical
    references and index.
Identifiers: LCCN 2016043218 (print) | LCCN 2016053861 (ebook) | ISBN
    9780749479657 (alk. paper) | ISBN 9780749479664 (ebook)
Subjects: LCSH: Information technology–Management.
Classification: LCC HD30.2 .R686 2017 (print) | LCC HD30.2 (ebook) | DDC
    658.4/038–dc23
LC record available at https://lccn.loc.gov/2016043218

Typeset by Graphicraft Limited, Hong Kong
Print production managed by Jellyfish
Printed and bound by CPI Group (UK) Ltd, Croydon, CR0 4YY

CONTENTS

ABOUT THE AUTHORS

Daniel Rowles has been working in Digital Marketing for nearly 20 years, with extensive experience working both client side and within the agency environment. He is a Course Director for the CIM, a certified Google Squared trainer and a Lecturer at Imperial College and Cranfield School of Management. Daniel has helped organizations of all types to use digital marketing effectively, working with a wide range of businesses, from start-ups through to global clients like the BBC, Sony, Tesco, British Council, Mercedes, L'Oreal and Warner Bros. He is the voice of the Digital Marketing Podcast, a worldwide top-10 business podcast in iTunes, CEO of TargetInternet.com and an award-winning author for publisher Kogan Page (Mobile Marketing, 2013, Digital Branding, 2014).

Daniel's training and consultancy is backed up by many years of real world experience planning and implementing digital campaigns. Daniel prides himself on his practical and hands-on training content, and brings best practice from many years working for a broad range of International clients across the full range of digital marketing techniques. His career has covered both the technical and business aspects of digital marketing, meaning he is able to bridge the gap between the two and make best use of the tools and technology available.

Thomas Brown is a consultant, executive advisor and prolific writer who's passionate about marketing, brand, digital and content.

Since 2016 he's been consulting for a number of organizations across financial services, education, non-profit, media and marketing services, advising leaders and teams on a range of issues from content strategy, brand journalism and customer experience strategy, to digital engagement, go-to-market strategy and market positioning... and helping to make implementation happen.

Alongside this, he entertains his love of words, writing for several brands, as well as special report features in The Times. He's also Chair of the Jury for the UK's Property Marketing Awards.

Prior to this he was the board-level Director of Strategy and Marketing at CIM, the world's leading professional body for marketing, where he focused on understanding the changing nature of marketing, building compelling thought leadership programmes, driving a distinct and authentic brand voice and leading the conversations that matter.

In more than 13 years at CIM, he was the architect of more than 35 major international research initiatives ranging from digital and social strategy to brand experience, marketing confidence to marketing capability... and lots more. He's an accomplished conference speaker and media commentator, and his words, ideas and work have been covered on, in and by The Financial Times, The Times, The Guardian, The Independent, Marketing, Marketing Week, Bloomberg and BBC News.

You can find him on Twitter attempting to be humorous, insightful or both @ThinkStuff and online at www.iamthinkstuff.com.

CONTRIBUTORS TO THIS BOOK

We'd like to thank the range of industry leaders who took part in the interviews which helped to shape this book, for their time, candid insights and invaluable guidance. You'll see some of their comments quoted in a range of chapters, but their wisdom and ideas permeate the whole book, even if not mentioned by name.

Ian Morgan, Managing Director, UK Digital Channels, **Barclays**

Will McInnes, Chief Marketing Officer, **Brandwatch**, @willmcinnes

Charles Yardley, Chief Operating Officer, **CityAM**

Caitlin Blewett, Director, Head of Digital, **Deloitte UK** @caiteblewett

Ciaran Rogers, Host of the **Digital Marketing Podcast** @ciaraniow

Eva Appelbaum, Partner, **Digital Talent @ Work** @evaapp

Ash Roots, Director of Digital, **Direct Line Group** @AshRoots

Simon Thompson, Global Head of Digital Commerce, **HSBC PLC**

Joe Petyan, Executive Partner, **J Walter Thompson London** @YuriEuro

Kristof Fahy, Chief Marketing Officer, **Ladbrokes plc** @kpf1970

Julien Callede, Co-Founder and Chief Operating Officer, **Made.com** @JulienCallede

Martin Fewell, Director of Media and Communications, **The Metropolitan Police** @martinfewell

Adam Stewart, Global Digital Director, **RB plc** @adster1

Russ Shaw, Founder, **Tech London Advocates** @RussShaw1

Dominic Grounsell, Global Marketing Director, **Travelex** @DomGrounsell

Gordon Nardini, Senior Director, Marketing, **Travelport** @flufforfact

Dara Nasr, UK Managing Director, **Twitter** @DaraNasr

Steven Zuanella, Group Chief Digital Officer, **RSA Insurance**

FOREWORD

It's no longer good enough to think of how you *do* digital – you have to *be* digital. It's all-consuming. Think you can hive it off to another part of the company or put the 'd' word in someone's title and still be successful? You're wrong.

Digital has created new markets and disrupted legacy ones. Challenged the status quo for long-established organizations and unlocked burgeoning new start-up economies all around the world. It's opened up new and better ways for people and brands to be a part of the conversations that matter, and offers businesses of all shapes and sizes the chance to be more efficient and more effective in pursuit of growth.

We all know that the world's largest taxi company owns no taxis, and the largest accommodation provider no real estate – digital is a business in its own right. We're living with Gen Z (those aged 1–20), the first generation to be tech innate, having grown up with mobiles and the internet from birth. Today, a third of all retail happens online, compared to just 1 per cent in 2000.

These facts bear out the importance of this book for any organization because this change isn't going to slow down, and its implications for your brand will only become greater. In the minute or two it takes you to read this foreword, as many as 7,000 tweets will have been sent – up to half a billion a day. And that's just the conversation on Twitter. Add in the multitude of other platforms and new technologies, and it's irrefutable that digital has fundamentally changed not only how society functions, but critically the relationship that brands need to have with their customers.

This is an exciting time where the scale of opportunity is unmatched in modern economic history. And that opportunity comes with an unrelenting pace of change that's only set to continue. To position yourself for success against this backdrop means getting the organizational conditions right – and building a digital culture is at the very forefront of this.

Dara Nasr, Managing Director, Twitter UK | @DaraNasr

ACKNOWLEDGEMENTS

Since this is my third book, I have exhausted my witty thank yous in the previous two. We've listed all of you who so kindly contributed and gave your time so generously in a separate section. It only leaves me to say that I owe the creation of this book, and most other good things in my life, to my beautiful and very talented wife Susana.

Daniel | @DanielRowles

There's a few people who've encouraged and supported me in writing this book, that deserve a hat tip here.

Firstly, to my former boss Anne Godfrey, without whose Virgo-moments over several years working together, this book would be 10 times as long. To a few of my former team, who not only tolerated me as a boss, but have also continued to do so as friends through 2016, each getting consistently better at feigning interest in what I'm writing about. Josie Burrell, Ben Pettifer, Krisztina Ustinov, Sammy Todd – expect to be quizzed on the book by page reference, shortly after publication.

To Cesar (however he pronounces it) Lastra of bash+build for the unending encouragement. To Freddie Ossberg, CEO of Raconteur Media for letting me write in *The Times* (and the candid critique along the way). And to Trevor Isherwood of Isherwood+Co, and Nick Hughes, top marketing dog at SEGRO plc, for the beer and the opportunities this year.

A quick mention of my dear friends Johanne Whittington, Julian Bier, Annika Haynes, Harriet Matthews, Amy ZS and Laura Smith, who have – whether or not they realize it – kept me sane during the months I've worked on this book, providing often-needed distraction.

Lastly, a massive thanks to my co-author Daniel Rowles for the boozy lunch that led to this collaboration, and his tireless support and patience of me throughout this journey. You've been #awesome.

Space simply won't allow me to keep going, so I'd like to close by making special mention of the rest of you. You know who you are.

Thomas | @ThinkStuff

To all the Rowlesosaurusie who make my life so happy:
Susana, Teresa, Charlie, Martin and guest
Rowlesosaurusie Luisa.
Daniel | @DanielRowles

To safeguard my inheritance, I dedicate my first book to
Margaret and Frank, my wonderful parents. After all,
they did teach me how to write.
Thomas | @ThinkStuff

Introduction

This book aims to answer a fairly simple question: How can our organizations succeed when the environment they operate in is changing so quickly?

Part One: Why you need a digital culture

Part One walks you through the range of factors that have led us to the fast-changing environment we find ourselves in. It explores the technology behind the change and in turn explains what this means for our organizations. As well as helping us understand the present, this Part also prepares us for a future in which the pace of change will increase, and in which organizations will not survive unless they are prepared for constant change.

Part Two: Plotting your digital journey

In Part Two we explore what it takes to make digital transformation happen, and lay the foundations for implementing an effective digital culture. We explore what digital really means for an organization, provide you with questions to help analyse your digital change priorities, explore how to go about undertaking a transformation, and explore the different strategies you can employ to position your organization for success.

Part Three: The Digital Culture Framework

Part Three gives you a structured framework of all of the things you will need to consider to build an organization that is operating in a constantly changing environment. This Part works as both a checklist, but also as a reference and guide that you revisit as you take on the particular challenges involved.

Part Four: Keeping up with change

Part Four looks at what happens once you have been through the process. We explore the techniques and approaches that will prevent you from lapsing back into previous approaches and how you can filter the ongoing change to work out what is important and what's not. Most importantly, this Part will explore how other organizations have dealt with the most common pitfalls and problems, so we can avoid the same challenges.

Epilogue

In this brief penultimate section, the authors offer some personal perspective from the more than 200 hours of interviews used to help with the book as they explore the key areas we should be absolutely focused on.

Appendix: The Digital Culture Toolkit

Building a digital culture is a challenging and ever-changing task. As such we have built a library of resources to help you along the journey, including frameworks and templates you can use straight away. However, since the pace of change continues unabated, you'll also find this online resource updated with the latest news and industry insights.

PART ONE
Why you need a digital culture

The increasing pace of change

Since you have just picked up a book on digital culture, it is probably already pretty clear to you we live in a time of increasingly rapid change. The reality is, that change has created huge business opportunity, but in at least equal measure it has created some huge business challenges. The average life expectancy of a company has dropped from around 67 years in the 1920s (Coase, 1937) to around 10 years now (Iyengar, 2016). This should be a very sobering thought for anyone in business. The company that you toil and work so hard to make succeed is statistically unlikely to exist in a decade.

> The average lifetime of a company has dropped from around 67 years in the 1920s to around 10 years.

Before we panic too much, the flip side of this is that we now have incredible organizations doing incredible things that we couldn't even imagine a decade ago. The other thought that may help us sleep at night is that the world's most valuable company, Apple Inc., is actually now 40 years old. However, the second most valuable company, Alphabet (the parent company for Google) is not even 12 months old at the time of writing, and Google itself is only 18 years old. Can you imagine trying to run an organization without being able to Google stuff? I am apparently old enough to remember this, but it seems an entirely foreign concept already.

Disruption

Industry after industry has been disrupted by technology in recent years. The music and movie industries actively tried to stick to their traditional business models while their customers around them completely changed how they consumed the media that was being sold. The disruption in both industries has been fast and it has been complete; the majority of teenagers no longer watch television in the traditional sense (Coughlan, 2016). If those teenagers are your target market and you haven't adapted, you're dead. Maybe you don't care about the teenage market. Soon enough those teenagers are your adult market and if you haven't adapted, you're dead. Besides, every market is changing, and even if not completely, by a significant enough percentage to hit your bottom line if you don't adapt.

If we read the official academic definition of marketing, it becomes pretty clear that active resistance to market changes is completely insane. The Chartered Institute of Marketing tells us: 'Marketing is the management process responsible for identifying, anticipating and satisfying customer requirements profitably.' (CIM, 2016). But many industries, when technological disruption comes along, attempt to actively resist customer requirements. Customers have decided they want something different and the company's reaction is to ignore the change and carry on regardless. However, in many cases the organizations may not be actively resisting, but the catch-up time between market change and company change is just too great.

Death by a thousand cuts

If it were just the occasional radical market change that was the problem, we would stand a chance of catching up. After all, even slow-moving companies can adjust and change given time, if there is a will to do so (and the will to change is incredibly important, and unfortunately, very often missing as we will discuss later in this book). However, the problem is that as soon as one change has happened another comes along, and we haven't even adjusted to the first one yet. And then another comes along, and the first change is still not complete, all of our budget is allocated and we are not selling as well as we did, so we also make cutbacks in new projects. Over a very short period of time, this cycle is lethal. Not only are revenues probably being hit, but it very often leads to poor morale as the stresses of failing projects and falling revenues compound one another. This in turn leads to staff churn, making the problem even worse.

The radical solution in these downward spirals is very often a sudden change of leadership: a new, steady hand to get everyone back inline. However, when this change in leadership, after a short honeymoon period of positive thinking, also leads to very similar results, we are now even further in trouble. What we really need is radical change throughout every aspect of the organization.

Digital transformation

Understanding the core concepts behind digital transformation is essential to stop this cycle that leads to company mortality. Digital transformation is the process of making our organization fit for purpose in a radically changed environment. However, not only is the environment radically changed, but it will continue to change, and we need the ability to keep pace with this change.

Digital transformation – yet another buzz term?

Digital transformation has all the signs of being a buzz term. It is mentioned at pretty much every business conference you will go to right now, consultants are offering expensive services to do it for you and most people don't really understand what it is. This combination leads to a fair bit of natural cynicism on the topic. However, just like many things that are difficult within business, it is also too easy to dismiss the topic. In reality digital transformation is a phrase that means many things to different people, but at its heart it is about making our organizations effective in fast-changing environments.

Beyond capability

Very often we will judge our current state of ability to operate in our current environment by looking at our 'Digital Capability'. Digital capability is a list of topics that we need to consider when going through a transformation project. This might include things like IT and technical infrastructure, resources and measurement. Very often on this list we see the word 'culture' as a standalone heading. The reality is that we can't just isolate this element of the transformation process, it affects every element of what we do.

Culture is the sum of the values, behaviours and 'norms' of those in your organization – which supports you today and may end up inhibiting your progress tomorrow. As we build an argument for a structured approach to building an effective digital culture, you will see that culture impacts everything else we do, and that is why the best way to deal with constant change is a change in culture.

The technology 02
catalyst

One of the main drivers in the pace of change that is creating so many opportunities and challenges is the exponential growth of computing power. As computing power increases and devices get physically smaller, what our computers (and therefore mobile devices) can do becomes more and more interesting. Advances like better voice recognition, augmented and virtual reality (AR and VR) and high-resolution video displays have all relied on these increases in computing power to make them available on mainstream mobile devices.

Enter Moore's Law

Moore's Law is an often quoted, but quite often not fully understood, observation in regard to the exponential growth of computing power made back in 1965. Gordon E Moore, co-founder of Intel, observed that the number of transistors on integrated circuits doubled roughly every two years.

These changes have a direct impact on the speed at which computers can process information, how much storage they can have in a given space, and are even connected to things like the potential resolution of your digital camera.

This means that computing power grows at an exponential rate (more on that later).

Moore's Law has proved to be exceptionally accurate; although he originally predicted that it would hold true for around 10 years, it has now done so for nearly 50 years.

The future of Moore's Law

There has been much discussion about the fact that Moore's Law cannot continue to hold true forever. Practically speaking, you can only have so many transistors in a physical space before you reach the limit of what is possible due to the limitations of physics.

However, if you look at Moore's Law more broadly, and think in terms of computing power, rather than transistors, there is a clear argument in favour of it holding true. What generally happens, when one technology reaches the limits of what can be done with it, is that some form of innovation is found to continue the progress of technology. Whether that's an entirely new material, manufacturing process or brand new technology, there are lots of examples of innovation allowing Moore's Law to continue when it looked to be reaching its limits.

Exponential growth in perspective

One of the most important elements of this growth in computing power that is impacting our mobile devices is its exponential rate. The human brain is very good at understanding things that grow in a linear way, that is, something that grows at the same rate on an ongoing basis, like counting from 1 to 100. What we are not so good at is getting our heads around exponential growth. The best way to do this is to consider an example.

I first heard the following analogy from my friend, and expert digital strategist, Jonathan Macdonald (look up some of his talks for some real inspiration on the future of technology). I have seen a number of different versions of the analogy online, but the key thing is to take note at the end of the story.

Filling a stadium with water, one drop at a time

Imagine a large stadium filling with water from a tap, one drip per minute, and imagine that stadium to be watertight so that no water could escape. If the tap continued dripping water in the same regular (linear) way, it would take many thousands of years to fill the stadium.

However, if that tap were dripping at an exponential rate, so that the number of drips coming out of the tap doubled every minute, it would be a very different story. The first minute there would be one drop, the second minute there would be two drops, the third minute four drops, the fourth minute eight drops and so on. This is exponential growth in action.

▶

Now imagine you are sitting on the seat at the very top of the stadium, with a view across the entire area. The first drop from the exponential tap is dropped right in the middle of the stadium field, at 12 pm. Remembering that this drop grows exponentially by doubling in size every minute, how much time do you have to leave the stadium before the water reaches your seat at the very top? Is it hours, days, weeks, months or years?

The answer is that you have exactly until 12.49 pm. It takes an exponential tap less than 50 minutes to fill a whole stadium with water. This is impressive but it gets more interesting. At what time do you think the football stadium is still 93 per cent empty? The answer: at 12.45 pm. So if you sat and watched the water level growing, after 45 minutes all you would see is the stadium field covered with water. Then, within four more minutes, the water would fill the entire stadium. It would then take one more minute to fill an entire other stadium. Exponential growth gets very big, very quickly.

Technology as an enabler

So let's consider what this growth in technology means in practical terms. It means that the devices we use will be able to do more and more things that previously seemed impossible, and the rate of these technology developments will get faster and faster.

You only have to look at technology development over the few decades to see this in practice. Thirty years or so ago, my iPhone would have looked like science fiction. (It should be noted, however, I still don't have a hover board.)

Recent innovations, such as real-time voice recognition language translation or controlling the playback of video by just looking at your television will seem like common technology in the near future.

This means that the increase in capabilities of the devices we use will enable us to do new things that we won't be currently thinking about. It is also likely that the role a mobile device takes in bridging the gap between the physical world and the online world will continue to grow.

The near future

Microsoft's HoloLens product (see Figure 2.1) is a glimpse of a very near future where augmented reality is commonplace. The product is already in existence and Microsoft, as well as external developers, is building and refining what it will be able to do.

Figure 2.1 Microsoft HoloLens: augmented reality wearable technology (www.microsoft.com/microsoft-hololens/)

Although HoloLens takes fairly widely available technologies, combines them and then wraps them in some clever software, it is causing a major reaction. This is in part due to the clever use of technology, but more about the idea of wearing technology and the idea of being 'constantly connected' and altering the reality around us.

Whenever I show HoloLens to a room full of students, delegates on a training course or an audience at a larger presentation, the audience seems to be divided between two points of view. One group of people is excited by the possibilities and impressed by the technology. The other group finds the prospect and implications of being able to change the reality around you disturbing.

Technology changing society

This reaction is interesting for many reasons, but most of all it shows how technology is changing our day-by-day lives so fundamentally. Essentially, the technology is moving more quickly than society is adapting to it and developing cultural norms in how to deal with it.

I see a great example of this every time I talk at a conference. A few years ago, if I was speaking on stage and somebody was looking down at their phone, it was a sign that I didn't have their attention. This may have been due to my talk being boring, them having more important things to deal with, or the fact that they weren't really interested in the first place. Now when I speak at a conference most people are looking down at their phones.

It may be that I am getting increasingly boring, but based on the level of tweets and social media posts, what they are actually doing is broadcasting snippets from my talk in real time. Increasingly the audience is also now live streaming from their devices. I am more than happy for what I am saying to be spread as widely as possible, but many event organizers are concerned. The audience in the room may have paid many hundreds or thousands of pounds to be there, but anyone on the appropriate social media channel can now watch the whole thing live, for free. Much as conference organizers might be terrified by this, the genie is not going back in the bottle.

Double-edged sword

This change in behaviour has both good and bad sides. Firstly, it is great because it means the members of the audience think there is value in what I am saying, enough value in fact to share it with their own, wider audience. That means in turn that I have a wider audience and will gain a larger social media following myself.

The downside is that it means the members of the audience are not fully listening to what I am saying and their engagement with my content may be fairly superficial: looking for sound-bites of content to publish, or streaming what I am saying without hearing it.

This double-edged sword is a reflection of two issues in my opinion. Firstly, we have not developed a culture around these kinds of circumstances yet to have worked out what is the best pattern of behaviour. If this change is hard for society to keep up with, no wonder organizations are struggling. Secondly, the technology is still getting in the way.

The ideal solution is not only a cultural one, where known behaviour is expected (for example, you turn your mobile off or to silent in the cinema), but also one of better technology. Technology that did not require me to look down at my mobile device and use my hands to interact with it would mean that posting social media updates would be far less interruptive.

Frictionless technology

Reducing how much the technology gets in the way of what I am trying to do and creating a more seamless experience is what 'frictionless' technology is all about. We could compare what technology we need to carry now to create, edit and publish a video. Twenty years ago it would have meant a lot of heavy and very expensive equipment. Now it means carrying the average smartphone.

The reaction HoloLens has created because of its wearable nature and the fact that it overlays something onto our 'real world' will become more and more relevant in the very near future. As mobile technology develops, the device itself becomes less and less relevant, and the utility it offers has the opportunity to be more and more frictionless. This again, however, means a faster pace of change.

Some fairly obvious examples come to mind very easily if you just look at HoloLens. Once the technology gets in the way less, how about not needing a headset at all? How long will it be until we have augmented reality contact lenses?

How about taking the experience of watching somebody on stage giving a presentation and trying to make the follow-up actions simpler? Using facial recognition you could automatically be shown the speakers' online profiles, previous work and other similar experts. Another example scenario could be that you have gone for a walk in the woods and see a snake. Your augmented reality contact lenses could identify the snake, take a picture and post it to your social networks to share your experience, and most importantly, tell you if it is dangerous or not.

The point is that it is so easy to think of a thousand day-to-day experiences that could be enhanced in some way by using these kinds of technologies. And all of these changes in our everyday experiences will mean that technology becomes more and more personal. You only need to have lost your phone once to realize that we are increasingly reliant and connected to the devices we use.

Privacy and the future of technology

One of the key features demonstrated in an early Google Glass (Google's original augmented reality glasses) promotion video (which showed a mock-up of its expected functionality rather than what it could actually do at that time) was the wearer of the device asking where his friend was, and his friend's location being immediately shown on the augmented reality display. This particular piece of functionality was always the one that seemed to draw the biggest gasps from an audience because of the implications this could have on privacy. The reality is that smartphone-based geographic location data has been around for some time, but its usage is

▶

one of the many things about sharing so much data that is increasingly concerning people.

The key issue at play is that of value exchange and transparency. If I share data with you, am I fully aware of that fact and do I know what you will do with that data? The other question, which consumers are increasingly asking, is: What do you offer me in exchange?

A clear value exchange proposition is going to become increasingly important when we attempt any form of marketing. If I give you my data, what functionality, or other value, will you give me in exchange? Then finally, and most importantly, do I trust you enough to give you my data?

The distant future

Really this section should be entitled 'The future seems distant, but will actually probably be a lot sooner than we think'. It is not all that catchy though, so we will stick with 'distant future'. If we go back to the exponential growth analogy of filling a stadium with water, we can see that the rate of change got pretty radical pretty quickly.

This could mean some very significant changes to the world around us. A very clear point, in my opinion, is the idea that 'mobile technology' will become irrelevant (and some would argue it already is). The integration of technology into everything we do, and even into us as human beings, will mean that the funny little devices we carry around now will in the future seem like the Dark Ages do to us now.

Consider that it is a fairly logical train of thought, that we will all be constantly connected to the internet (whatever that looks like then!), wherever we go. It is also not unreasonable to think that computing power and artificial intelligence will have radically advanced and machines will be far more 'intelligent'. (When you start to consider that sentient life may not be limited to organic organisms, we start to get a little too science fiction for the remit of this book, I'm afraid). It is also a fairly logical path that would lead us to believe we can control and interact with devices by thinking, since you can already get games that allow you to use your brain waves to control physical objects (MindWave from NeuroSky).

These relatively logical progressions of technology mean that the world we live in will be radically changed. I find this extremely exciting and feel very blessed to live in such fast-changing times. If, however, this all fills you with a sense of dread, bear in mind it is the application not the technology that is the issue. When video cassettes first came into usage by the general population, there were huge concerns about 'video nasties'. We adjusted and the world continued.

A guaranteed future prediction

The only guarantee is that the pace of change within the arena of digital technology, and the rate at which this impacts our organizations and wider society, will get faster and faster. Organizations (and individuals) that are able to adapt to ongoing change will be best placed to survive and thrive in this environment. That is why we need a digital culture.

New channels, 03 tools and business models

The technology innovations that are driving the pace of change we have been discussing amplify one another in unpredictable ways. This amplification can mean a small advance or innovation in technology can have huge repercussions. Let's start with a simple example and look at how this change, combined with the right circumstances, can disrupt entire industries.

In 2009–10 Apple and Google introduced 'push notifications' to their mobile operating systems. This meant that we could have multiple apps running at once, and these apps could update us when something had, or was about to happen. Push notifications was a relatively linear progression in the development of mobile operating systems. It was certainly new, but very few of us would have imagined what a shift this would have led to. Now think what start-ups, developers and business entrepreneurs have done with this technology. Need a taxi right now? Just use Uber. Want delivery food from any restaurant in your city, even if they don't deliver, and want to see its progress in getting to you in real time? Just use Deliveroo. Want to learn a language and be motivated to log back in when you have been slacking off from your studies? Duolingo is for you, then. All of these apps would not have been possible without the simple innovation of push notification systems.

However, it is not just the technology changes themselves that have led to the current pace of change. Rising profits at companies like Apple, Facebook and Google, along with the incredible levels of competition between these companies, have led to huge investments in research and development, driving technology forward ever faster. We have also seen the growth of the 'start-up' world, where investors are putting huge amounts of money into companies that do not necessarily make any money yet, on a gamble they may become the next Snapchat, Uber or Airbnb. You do not need many of these bets to pay off to pay back your initial investment, especially when you consider these companies are currently estimated to be worth a total of US $109 billion (Austin *et al*, 2015)!

This huge growth in investment in start-ups has led to an environment very well suited to growing new and innovative companies quickly and has led to a generation of entrepreneurs keen to make their fortune by building new and fast-growing ventures. These entrepreneurs are actively looking for opportunities to disrupt markets, to change the status quo and to change customer expectations.

Business to business and technology innovation

On first inspection, the innovations that drive the world of start-ups and apps seem a long way from how the B2B world operates. Generally, the B2B world is risk averse, traditional and change happens more slowly.

The reality, however, is that every person who works in a B2B is also a consumer and operates in the same world we all do. Many of us use our mobile devices throughout the day, we shop online and we use social media to greater or lesser extents. This has all led to changing expectations. We expect faster response times, we expect quicker delivery and we expect personalization. This change in attitudes means that B2B organizations need to adapt and innovate just like all other organizations. And where industries are not keeping up, they risk the loss of market share to smaller and more agile new players. Even in industries like finance, where resistance to change and increased concerns about risk has led to a much slower level of change, new business models are now disrupting these industries. We discuss this in far more detail in the next section of this chapter.

New channels

Facebook was launched on 4 February 2004. In the first quarter of this year it had 1.65 billion users and made US $5.2 billion in advertising revenue in the same period (Seetharaman, April 2016). All very impressive numbers, and we could go on quoting them all day. The reality is that in just over a decade our media consumption has completely changed.

No matter what industry you work in, your target audience's media consumption will be changing and will continue to do so. To some extent, although the pace of change was slower, this has always been the case. We read newspapers, then there were more newspaper options, then came radio, then television, etc. We are probably aware of these changes, but what we generally do not have is any sort of mechanism for deciding when this media consumption change should trigger a change in how we plan activities like our marketing.

The flow of internal questioning normally goes something like this:

We know this new channel is growing, but our competitors are not using it yet so it does not matter yet, right?

Our competitors are using the new channel, but they are not getting engagement so it does not matter, right?

Our competitor has nailed this channel, why aren't we using it? Whose fault is this?

We need a digital culture to help us plan the process of review and initialization of testing new things out. We need a culture in which we are committed to constantly trying new things. Many organizations claim to have an innovation culture, where it is all right to fail. However, ask how many people in these organizations have run three unsuccessful projects in a row and got a job promotion. Not many, I am guessing. There is also another word in that previous sentence that prevents much innovation in many cases: the word 'project'. There is nothing intrinsically wrong with a project, but because of the way many of our organizations are structured, it means the word is associated with many other things. Things like sign-off and compliance, things like project team recruitment and worst of all, things like meetings. Lots and lots of meetings. All of these things are not necessarily bad (except the meetings), but they all slow down progress, so if we must have them, they need to be organized in such a way that they are as efficient and as effective as possible. Part Two and Part Three of this book will help you work through the process to achieve this.

New tools

I can tell you how many people are on my website right now in real time. I can tell you the countries they are in, how they got to my website and how long they are staying for. For any of you who use Google Analytics, this will come as no surprise. For those not so familiar, Google offers a free tool that will give all this information and far more. The problem is no longer a lack of data, but rather overwhelming data and not knowing what to do with it.

The myriad of tools available to us can actually cause decision paralysis. Overwhelmed by the options, we do not make any decisions, and we therefore collect no actionable data. Most organizations do use analytics, but purely from a reporting standpoint. Once a month someone holds up a chart that paints some good news and the meeting moves on to the next individual or department's turn. The individual or department is now vindicated for another month, but nothing had been learned or any real progress made. We need a culture and process that helps us measure the right things and makes sure we do it consistently. We need an atmosphere in which we can be curious and challenge the status quo to try new things and a culture of innovation that actively encourages failing, so we at least learn what does not work.

Very often, when I discuss this idea of adopting a culture that actively encourages failure, I am looked at with a combination of bewilderment and dismay. It is all very well telling people to go and fail, but if a company just keeps failing, surely the company itself will eventually fail! The point is we are not just trying random things to see if they fail, then moving on to something completely new. We are carefully selecting an area for experimentation based on the data or informed assumptions we have. Then if we fail we adjust our experiment until we identify the winning combination of factors that make our experiment a success.

Digital Culture Toolkit

To accompany the book, we have collected together a selection of tools and templates to assist you in building digital culture:

www.targetinternet.com/digitalculture

It is perfectly possible, if you adopt a culture of trying new things, without applying this more rigorous approach, to dismiss things as not working, when in reality you just have not applied them well. I see this happen again and again, and sadly very often with social channels that can have a huge impact. A company tries out a channel (and this happens on Twitter a lot sadly), sends out a few ill-thought-out and commercially focused tweets, and then does not see any immediate response. Due to the lack of immediate response, no great effort is put into the channel, with someone sending things out on an ad-hoc basis when they remember, just to make sure they have ticked something off their task list. Eventually some will ask, 'Did

Twitter work?', and the answer is 'No'. Not in any way because of Twitter, but in reality because of a complete lack of planning and application of best practice.

New business models

We have already mentioned a few brands like Uber and Airbnb, that have come up with completely new business models, and we will talk about these more in a moment. Before we do that, however, it is worth considering that we really do not need a new innovative business model to become successful. We could just do something better in some way. We could improve our product, our service, our customer service. But we must also consider that the demand for our product or service could die out at any time if our market is disrupted in some way. We need to consider how we can predict this disruption, stay ahead of it or even cause it ourselves (more on this in the next chapter)!

Now let's move back to these new business models and start with the obvious ones. Both Uber and Airbnb basically used technology to cut out the middleman. The old model was that if you wanted a taxi in a major city you needed to travel to a predefined pick-up spot, such as a taxi rank and then queue for a taxi. If none were available, you would wait, with no idea how long a taxi would be and with no way of notifying the taxi firm that you were there. Alternatively, you could flag a taxi down, assuming one would pass you at an opportune time. If it was raining you could forget it, as supply and demand just completely flipped and you now have no chance. Not only was this system completely broken, it was hugely inefficient for drivers. This inefficiency leads to higher than necessary fairs. Instead if you simply connect someone who wants a driver, with a driver who is nearby, and allow both parties to vet one another, the system is suddenly much more functional, efficient and cheaper.

As someone who spends most of my days in London, I am very clear on the opposing arguments. London's black cabs are iconic, the drivers have to pass extensive training so they know every road in London (it is an epic undertaking of learning known as 'The Knowledge') and have to drive a specific type of vehicle. They are the only vehicles you are legally allowed to flag down in London; all others must be pre-booked. Is Uber pre-booking or is it virtually flagging someone down? It is basically semantics and all it tells me is that the previous system's rules are not in line with the reality of modern London. To me the market will decide. Do I want to pay for a driver who knows where he is going or one who uses the sat nav? Do I want to be able to travel in exclusive lanes that can only be used by black cabs and buses, or do I think the slightly increased journey time is worth the money I will save? Do I think a black cab offers benefits that suit me rather than an Uber driver?

Soon there won't be any taxi drivers

I am not trying to give an exhaustive debate of the licensed taxis versus Uber argument. For example, Uber drivers are often paid very little, too many new cars in a city will increase congestion and most Uber cars do not offer wheelchair access, to highlight just a few arguments the other way. Also bear in mind, that in the very near future, we will have driverless cars and the argument will shift again. Uber has already said its intention is that its cars will be driverless in the future and Uber is working on the technology (BBC, 2016). You can read more about driverless cars in Chapter 21 on innovation.

The reaction to Uber has been interesting to say the least, and you can read a million different accounts online. However, my key observation would be, that every industry that I have seen resisting disruption by trying to keep the status quo has failed to do so and wasted huge amounts of time and resources in the process. Rather than crying foul, the incumbent needs to improve its offering and/or to clearly define what it offers and how it is differentiated from the new entrant. Or just give up now.

Airbnb has done the same for accommodation that Uber has done for transport. The existing system is incredibly inefficient. Running a hotel that is not constantly full is an expensive business, so the cost of staying there when you want to goes up. It is a lot cheaper to stay in someone's spare room. However, this is a trivialized argument. The two options are not plush hotel room or someone's spare room. I have stayed in terrible hotels and incredible Airbnb apartments. The point is that new business models are offering new alternatives and new competition, and if the existing market does not adjust to compete for the audience, the very best that can be hoped for is a loss in market share.

Beyond Uber

It is easy to get bogged down talking about the Ubers of the world, but what about smaller scale new business models? Buying groceries is a great example. First of all we had great big out of town grocery stores. But before long we didn't all want to drive to get our groceries and we moved to buying little and often, so we got the smaller convenience store type supermarket. Next we adopted online shopping and it seemed that the supermarkets' problems were coming to an end. Then suddenly the market has been flooded with new competitors. Not new supermarkets with big expensive overhead stores, but new online-only suppliers. Some of these new suppliers even have their own super-efficient infrastructure in place; Amazon now delivers groceries and people like what they are doing.

As well as big players like Amazon attacking the market, there are a hundred smaller services. For example, both Gousto and HelloFresh allow you to order regular boxes of preselected fresh ingredients with everything you need to cook their recipes. All of this chips away at market share for the major supermarkets unless they can innovate themselves.

Free is always cheaper

One of the scariest scenarios for most organizations is that of a competitor doing what you do for free. Google purchased a commercial analytics package called Urchin and gave it away for free. So what is the business model here? Well, having good web analytics will help you improve your website and an improved website is more likely to drive conversions, that is, get people doing the things you want them to do. If your website is converting, you can justify ad spend and how does Google make most of its money? By selling ads.

What about open source software that is given away for free? How does that make money? My favourite example of this is Wordpress. Wordpress in a free, open source (meaning its code is available to anyone who wants it), content management system (CMS). Wordpress now powers more than 26 per cent of all the world's websites (Wordpress, 2016). So how can you make money giving something away for free? You simply sell premium services, such as hosting and development for high-end customers. Not only is this an approach that has driven value, with a current valuation for Automattic (the corporate face of Wordpress) of US $1.2 billion (Best, 2016), but it has also driven huge brand advocacy. People love Wordpress and they are passionate about it. You can buy Wordpress Babygros and Christmas decorations. Seriously.

No one would pay for a service they could get for free, surely? Well actually they would, and probably with good reason. Plenty of people do not use Google Analytics or Wordpress and they may have good reason, but that is not my point. People are willing to pay for premium, for filtering or for any other perceived value. Most of us have attended a training course at some point or another. I am almost 100 per cent sure that you could have learned everything in that course by using Google, had you been willing to put in the time and effort. However, what we are paying for is filtering, convenience and hopefully effectiveness. Just because something is currently free, does not mean you cannot charge for it, and just because it is paid for does not mean you cannot give it away for free.

Another dot com bubble?

If you have the dubious pleasure of being my age or older, you may remember the first dot com bubble bursting. For those of you who don't, a very quick recap. Back in the late 1990s the internet boom occurred. Lots of companies that did not yet make any money, or at least certainly were not profitable yet, started to be given huge valuations and the 'bubble' grew. Then soon after the turn of the new millennium, the bubble burst and many of the companies that had been built mainly on speculation of what was possible, went bust and completely disappeared. One of the more high-profile cases was Pets.com, a pet supplies online retailer, which had over US $300 million invested into it that completely vanished. However, less well remembered for this early period of the internet was that companies like Amazon and eBay survived this first bubble bursting.

Since this massive loss in confidence and investment in the early parts of the 21st century, there have always been rumblings of us heading in that direction again. Facebook was not profitable initially, and the bubble conversations began again in earnest. Instagram was purchased by Facebook for US $1 billion when it had never made a single cent in revenue and the conversations intensified. The reality is that Facebook is now hugely profitable.

Many of the start-ups that are invested in fail to make a profit and many do not exist a year after starting. So, is this a bubble? My opinion, and just like any financial prediction it is just that, is that this is no way a bubble. The value of being invested in, in the early stages of an organization that may change the world cannot be overstated. Sure, some of the valuations may be over the top, but everything we are discussing points us towards companies that can leverage the change all around us, as having a great opportunity to succeed.

Why organizations really fail at digital

04

The disciplines and channels of digital (what we generally refer to as digital marketing) are not actually all that complicated. There is certainly lots to learn to become an expert in search engine optimization (SEO), social media and effective e-mail marketing, but it definitely is not rocket science. So if this is the case, why do so many organizations struggle so much when trying to implement digital channels and tactics?

The reality is that although the implementation of the tactics themselves is not too complicated, the surrounding issues that need to be resolved to implement effectively are anything but simple. This involves things like getting the appropriate management buy-in, getting your IT infrastructure working correctly and having the appropriate skills and team structure required. All of these things are complicated and involve lots of change. In order to develop a digital culture that allows you to effectively implement your digital channels, there are going to be lots of change projects and lots of IT projects. Universally, companies have always been bad at two things: change and IT. This is why organizations really fail at digital.

Changing external landscape

The realization that digital requires complex, carefully managed change and, potentially, large IT projects, has led to a number of fundamental changes in the market that deliver related services. Originally, we had a market with lots of agencies that delivered digital marketing services, such as SEO, social media, e-mail marketing, and so on. It soon became apparent, though, that it was not always easy to implement these projects without some initial changes being made within the organization. Digital agencies were not always best prepared to assist with this change process, but those that were started to offer digital transformation related services. Those that could not offer these services, and could not partner with somebody that could, often found that although they could offer great advice, it often was not possible to implement it, and eventually they would lose clients.

At this stage, organizations not traditionally associated with digital marketing started moving into the space. These were organizations that had identified that what was really needed was change management consultancy and large-scale IT projects, and these organizations had been doing these kinds of things for many years. Big global firms like Accenture, Deloitte, Cap-Gemini, EY, PwC and KPMG all started offering digital consulting services, not only to address digital marketing-related topics, but more broadly digital topics like cloud infrastructure, smart operations, mobile workforces and so on. This shift has helped speed the progress of many organizations to move to an effective digital culture. However, an experienced and well-trusted partner is not a key to guaranteed success. We still need an appropriate starting point and expectations internally.

Changing internal landscape

Dave Chaffey is a well-respected digital marketing author (as well as being an excellent lecturer, public speaker and someone whose opinion I respect). He runs a website called SmartInsights.com that provides digital marketing advice and stimulates conversation on the topic. As such he regularly asks his audience how many of them are carrying out any form of digital marketing and how many of them have a strategy behind this activity. Every time this questionnaire is run, the results come back the same. Nearly 70 per cent of those asked are carrying out digital marketing activities with no strategy. Although this is only a small sample survey, it does identify a key trend that I can back up from my many years of working with organizations to improve their digital marketing efforts.

Now, to be fair, this 70 per cent might be doing the right things, for the right reason, measuring effectively and achieving their business objectives. Although I am pretty sure that is not the case for all of them. Even if it, they probably would not know it, as they have no strategy to measure their success against.

So many organizations have no digital strategy, but what about those that do? Very often the digital strategy is not integrated or aligned with the overall marketing strategy and in turn this is not aligned with the business strategy. It makes no sense having a series of unaligned strategies, so once we have aligned these, our attention very often then moves towards understanding where digital fits within the organization.

Different aspects of digital are very often covered by our marketing and IT teams, so normally we find that much of our digital capability is focused there. We may have specialist teams or generalists, but we need to work out how these people can serve the needs of the entire organization, as and when we need to implement digital-related projects. This leads to the thorny questions of how we should structure our companies and teams, and I can say now, without a doubt, there is no single correct answer to the question. We explore this topic in detail in Part Three, but what we need to achieve is flexibility and agility, so that as our requirements change and shift, we are not limited and held back by our internal structure.

Broad skillsets

The environment we operate in is changing quickly, the companies that help service our organizations are changing and our organizational structures themselves are changing. So where does this leave the individuals within the organizations and how can they cope with all this change? We need different and broader skillsets than ever before and we need to be constantly updating our skills. We explore this extensively in Chapter 13, Skills and talent, of Part Three, but it is clear that a fast-changing environment needs people with the appropriate skills, the ability to change and an attitude that can embrace an uncertain and ever-changing future.

One of my favourite roles is teaching at Imperial College in London on their strategic marketing masters programme. Imperial is very often ranked as one of the top five universities in the world, and as such the entry requirements for students is very high, and therefore the students are a very smart and very motivated bunch. The best students from the course are aggressively recruited by many of the world's top companies, with several always ending up at Apple and Google. So what do we teach them that makes them so desirable to these great companies? One of the first things I take them through is the broad skillset they will need to be successful in the fast-changing environment they will be working in. This breaks down into four key areas:

1 Tactical knowledge of the channels and techniqes they will need to use directly or that will be used by the people they manage. If you have an agency carrying out tactical work for you, you need to know almost as much as the agency's staff to manage them effectively.

2 Strategic knowledge to effectively plan their activity.

3 Some IT knowledge so that technical factors do not become sticking points and so that they can manage the technical members of their team. This means that it is easier to earn these members of staff's respect, as well as minimizing them bamboozling you with reasons a project cannot be finished on time!

4 Interpersonal skills, so that they can get management buy-in, manage cross-disciplinary teams and work with people through times of uncertainty and uncomfortable change.

No one will be perfect at everything, and each individual has his or her own stronger and weaker skillsets, but there is one more thing that is not listed here, and something that it is not easy to teach. Individuals who thrive in the current environment of change have an attitude of flexible determination and curiosity. They want to be effective, they are always willing to explore new ways of delivering results and they are committed to ongoing learning.

Since attitudes are developed over time, internal morale and group attitudes will impact the individual. It therefore becomes essential that the organization is focused on its digital culture in order to create the right atmosphere to nurture and retain these individuals. Without the right individuals, the organization cannot build an effective digital culture.

Conclusions

As we can see, the core tactical elements of what we consider digital are not our main challenge. The main challenge is the huge range of supporting elements that need to be lined up to give an opportunity for success. We therefore need a comprehensive approach to make sure each element required is in place so that we cannot only implement our current plans, but also continue to evolve within our fast-changing environment. Part Three aims to be that comprehensive guide to the steps and best practices involved. Good luck!

The Digital Culture Framework

Part Three of this book gives you a structured framework of all of the things you will need to consider to build an organization that is operating in a constantly changing environment. It works best if you read the whole Part, so you see how each element fits together with the other parts. However, the Part also works as a reference guide that you revisit as you take on the particular challenges involved. The case study below should give you some perspective before you get going.

CASE STUDY   Digital transformation in action

Author: Eva Appelbaum, Partner, Digital Talent @ Work (formerly Head of Digital Marketing Transformation, BBC)

I took on a digital marketing transformation role a number of years ago when there was a real trend towards digital 'separation'. You would see Labs, or 'skunkworks' or other separate spaces where digital teams could operate without being hindered by the limitations of the existing business culture, policies, processes or technology. The idea was that this is how you accelerated digital maturity.

But I always saw problems with these models. Firstly, it set up a digital silo, and thus sent a message that digital was someone else's job, it was 'exclusive' or disconnected from the rest of the business. I never believed that. The other problem with these models is that at some point you have to address the existing business, existing employees. How could the business change if the change was taking place separately? How could people improve their digital skills, if digital responsibilities sat elsewhere?

So with this role, I thought I have two options: Either I set up a new digital silo that did cool digital things in hermetically sealed conditions, and yes I could deliver great digital work and yes my team could hone our skills and understanding, but would I actually be transforming anyone else? The other option was to try to come up with an 'embedded' alternative, which was all about changing the culture from within. And I was fortunate to find that marketers were extremely keen to embrace digital. Some of them were already brilliant digital marketers, who joined this organization only to feel completely discouraged by its daunting internal challenges. Others were more traditional marketers who were desperate to do more, but lacked the confidence or felt unsure of their own abilities. The appetite for change was most certainly there!

So I designed a model for digital transformation that called itself a Digital Marketing Lab (because I knew it needed a name!), but that wouldn't really be a Lab at all. Rather it would be embedded within the existing organizational structure, and instead of striving for shiny innovation, it would concentrate on sorting out some of the basics – helping marketers, and the business, improve digital capabilities.

I asked for just enough leeway to be able to circumvent some of the more cumbersome processes. I brought in a small team of consultants and established a network of external providers or agencies we could work with when necessary. I then let marketers know that they could come to us at any time for help, or advice or suggestions, or introductions. They could bring us real campaigns to work alongside them on, or real problems… anything really.

The idea was that this 'Lab' would be a taste of that elusive 'separate' digital space, coming to them. It would be a space where they could experiment with digital in a safe way, where they could get support and mentoring from digital experts, and where they could turn to when they needed help breaking down institutional barriers.

This 'Lab' was also different in that marketers owned their own projects, which meant that if things were successful they could take credit for them, and which in turn incentivized them to come to us. Our involvement could be as light-touch as just a bit of advice, or completely full-service with one of our digital lab members joining a campaign team.

We wanted them to work on digital campaigns themselves so that they could learn by doing, build up their own confidence and wouldn't need us anymore!

We worked in real, imperfect conditions, within existing structures, with existing technology and with all the usual limitations. But by doing so, we were able to uncover many of the blockers that had been hindering marketers from using digital channels, content or tactics in their campaigns. And, by uncovering these, we were able to make recommendations for wider, systemic changes so as to improve capabilities.

The Digital Marketing Lab was not aiming for ground-breaking innovation. But, I was certain we were providing the right innovation.

Lighting little fires and helping shift ways of working. Benchmarking achievements against the way things used to be.

The feedback we got for this approach was encouraging:

- *'Digital feels like a greater priority, and it's not just talk as the Digital Lab lends real support/inspiration/people power to get digital initiatives shifting.'*

- *'The Digital Lab encouraged and enabled me to think differently about how I approach digital – think this is true for many teams.'*

- *'It supports and eases the wheels for those wanting to do more.'*

- *'Injects enthusiasm and opportunity in the digital space – often people can feel daunted.'*

- *'There's a sense that we are actually trying to DO something about the challenges.'*

Nowadays received wisdom has evolved and digital transformation is generally expected to be embedded in the business. It is more common to question digital silos, or to question the need for 'digital' at all. Now we ask: isn't digital part of everyone's job? It's nice to think we were ahead of that curve!

PART TWO
Plotting your digital journey

What a digital transformation looks like   05

> Like air and drinking water, being digital will be noticed only by its absence, not its presence.

So wrote Nicholas Negroponte, Chairman of MIT Media Lab in a prescient article 18 years ago (Negroponte, 1998). Yes, that's not a typo. 1998. When most of us were still marvelling at the melodies of our dial-up 28.8kb modem (although I appreciate that some people reading this book will not know what that is – ask your parents).

Negroponte's beautifully simple statement sums up, for me, why organizations increasingly need to evolve their strategy and their business to be successful in today's constantly changing world. Digital technology has evolved from being a thing or a feature, to being part of the very fabric of the world we live and work in, yet for many organizations, it is still treated as 'a thing'.

Businesses have recognized this for one of several reasons. First, they might just have noticed the major shifts in customer and consumer behaviour driven by technology. Many of the staggering statistics we shared in the opening section of this book illustrate the scale and pace of change in the world, and too many businesses have been slower than their customers in response to this.

Second, businesses might have had their category or market disrupted, or witnessed the effects of disruption in other markets. Dollar Shave Club and razors. Uber and taxis. Airbnb and hotels. LinkedIn and recruitment. WhatsApp and messaging. Skype and phone calls. Amazon Dash and grocery shopping. Examples are plentiful and out of either blind fear or just good planning, businesses are trying to understand how to protect themselves from a future disruption (or how to become a disruptor).

It's not a matter of if, but when every business/category will be disrupted in some shape or form, and there are two ways that we tackle this challenge within our business. Firstly, we ensure we have the competent 'scouts' constantly reviewing the external landscape, understanding the movements of consumer behaviours/needs, businesses (start-up to enterprise), technology and innovative methodologies. Secondly, we ensure we build the internal capabilities, and most importantly the agility, to react to these movements, yet with an aim to be always the disruptors and not the disrupted. *Adam Stewart, Global Digital Director, RB plc | @adster1*

Third, they might be seeing new opportunities emerging within or around their business or sector that require new skills, technologies, capabilities or ways of working, and are keen to exploit these in the pursuit of growth. Or fourth, they might be witnessing changing or atypical competitor actions that they are struggling to make sense of. Lastly, it may be driven by the simple reality of business performance, be it customer churn, customer satisfaction or other fundamental indicators of the health and future prospects of your business.

Whatever the drivers are, organizations in general are facing up to the need to adapt to this constantly changing world, even if they don't necessarily know what the answer might be or how to get there. That's why digital transformations have become more commonplace, and why it's a hotly researched and discussed topic.

'The consumer packaged goods (CPG) industry are having to extend their thinking into very different new product development (NPD) and innovation to remain relevant in today's digitized and connected world. They are having to "think beyond the physical product" into services, artificial intelligence and machinery, alongside innovative new business models with new revenue streams.

'As part of the war of "who owns the consumer", the CPG industry simply needs to reconnect with the consumer to strengthen their chance of survival. They need to offer attractive value exchanges to consumers, giving the business the opportunity to reconnect and deepen relationships over a life-long term. Connected Innovations is just one strategy they will use to reconnect with the consumer. So what are the disruptive connected innovations, digital services and new business models we could create from brands like Nurofen, Durex, Dettol and even Finish? The mind goes wild, yet you'll have to wait and see...

'A very strong example to explain this new thinking required is Under Armour, another traditional physical product-based business (UA performance apparel). They recently acquired MyFitnessPal, Endomondo and MapMyFitness, three digital services, paying over US $700 million. Now they have a very strong connected "known" audience, right down to an individual level.

'It is claimed to be the biggest community of fitness, health and nutrition in the world. With over 160 million unique registered users and over 75 million active monthly users interacting at high frequency, this gives Under Armour their own marketing engine to cross-sell apparel, alongside powerful insight and the opportunity for new revenue streams through the new digital currency of data – all being services. These acquisitions have taken them from being just a physical product manufacturer to being a connected business with strong connection with consumers. A great example of what a digital transformation for an organization like ours – and other traditionally physical product-based businesses – might involve.'

Adam Stewart, Global Digital Director, RB plc | @adster1

What does a digital transformation involve?

The term 'digital transformation' has become rather fashionable over recent years, and can be used to describe anything from making and building a new website to changing your business model, and an awful lot in between. We look in detail at how you can define what digital transformation means for your business in Chapter 9, but it is worth first dispensing some of the hype that is so common in much of the marketing and digital world.

Managing change and stakeholders

First of all, transformation involves change. And change needs managing, or it manages you. That means you will need to understand how people think and behave, and if you are embarking on a large-scale transformation, consider the psychology of change.

You will need to be savvy to the different needs, priorities, objections and definitions of success for a range of different stakeholders, both internal and external. You will need to be attuned to how your organization's decisions and actions have an impact on different departments, teams and stakeholders and be proactive in managing any fallout from that.

Building a plan

A digital transformation initiative is not some form of dark art that requires a revolutionary new approach to building a plan. As with many things in business, the basic principles of analysis, consideration and robust planning apply.

First you need to understand where you are starting from. You need to know the context your organization is facing (your external environment, any threats or opportunities) and your internal capabilities (your strengths and weaknesses).

You need some clear goals or objectives to define what you are trying to achieve and give you an opportunity to evaluate progress and performance. You then need to set out how you are going to achieve them in light of the position you are starting from.

It is really that simple. Where are we now? Where do we want to get to? How are we going to get there? What are the key steps we will take? Who is responsible for doing what? How will we measure success?

In the world of marketing, this is often referred to as the SOSTAC planning framework. This does not mean you need to spend days or weeks in war rooms and the outcome does not need to be a lengthy planning document that never again sees the light of day, or a suite of strategy presentations with complex models and charts. Planning is a thought process, not a document, and it is going through the steps that is more important than what the output looks like.

Being adaptive

You will also need to be able to adapt. Whatever specifics you are setting out to achieve with your efforts to transform your organization into a truly digital business, one thing you can guarantee is that things will change during your journey.

The central idea behind this book, and the reason that organizations need to develop a digital culture, is to help them survive and thrive in a constantly changing environment. Embarking on a change initiative does not put external forces in a holding pattern until you have completed your endeavours.

Competitors will still act. Market forces will still change. And there will be ripple effects from the things you do, change and launch that mean you will need to be responsive, agile, and able to pivot or course-correct along the way.

Digital transformation is not a nice little neat box that you tick. It's a fundamental and existential business question.

It's a *business* challenge, it's about *business* transformation. And it's existential because some industries have been disrupted already, while others like ours haven't yet but they're on the road, and it's just a question of when, not if. This is a leadership challenge. It's not a technical challenge or a marketing challenge. It's a leadership challenge from the top – don't dismiss it or pigeon hole into an IT department, because a lot of people put digital transformation into IT, and say, 'Right, go and find me some systems that are going to enable me to do even better.' That's not going to work for the transformations that I believe organizations need. *Steven Zuanella, Group Chief Digital Officer, RSA Insurance*

'However your organization chooses to approach a digital transformation, one of the most common challenges arises when you lose sight of what your customers are doing. Not what they're doing out in the world, but how they consume media or how they want to consume media.

'Consider how much customer service has changed. Not that many years ago, your options for raising a complaint or asking for help came in the form of a letter or a phone call. Today, you might tweet a brand in seconds, rather than writing letters or emails, or listening to hold music. The challenge for businesses is keeping up and managing expectations. When I joined Twitter a few years ago, some companies' Twitter pages would read "This is not our Customer Service channel. For Customer Support, please visit our website". Customers would be left heading to a website, facing five or six different clicks to find a phone number, and then sitting on hold for an operator. Fifteen or 20 minutes later that customer could be rather disaffected. With the number of customers turning to social media for help and support, this can't continue to be ignored.

'To address this expectation gap, companies have to understand that whilst real-time and immediacy of response are great in practice, managing expectations is key. Take KLM for an example. Their Twitter page will display up-to-date information on response times from their social support channels. Sometimes it can be just a few minutes; other times, when the pressure is on, it might be 30 minutes. Customers don't tend to object to what the response time is, so long as their expectations are managed. Knowing you can tweet your airline and pop away for half an hour and do something else is a better feeling than sitting waiting for a reply.

'Problems arise when you don't see these customer behaviour changes going on around you. Losing sight of how your customers are interacting with different media and channels, or worse, just ignoring the signals, can be more than problematic. That said, not all change has to be large-scale and you don't have to make quantum shifts to be successful. Many businesses are already successful in their own right, so why should they have to suddenly change overnight? It's better to think about it and have a proper strategy than just do something for the sake of it, because other businesses are doing it.'

Dara Nasr, Managing Director, Twitter UK | @DaraNasr

Lessons learned

During the research for this book, we interviewed a wide range of senior industry professionals, many of whom you will see input or comments from throughout this book. One of the questions we posed to many of them who had been through or were midway through a digital transformation programme, was this: 'If you could go back to the genesis of this initiative, what advice would you give yourself or what would you approach differently and why?'

As you think about how your organization might need to adapt to be successful in this constantly changing world, we thought it might be helpful to share some of the reflections from those who have already trodden a similar path.

Ian Morgan, Barclays

'Two things that spring to mind. Firstly, I recently presented to our CEO and Executive Committee, and took them through a set of customer experience principles that we needed the organization to buy into if we were really going to achieve a step change in delivering value to our customers through digital platforms. These governing principles included things like "we design for mobile first and launch on mobile first", "we will have a single destination site not siloed microsites", among others. Getting the whole of the ExCo to understand and commit to these principles has been a real step forward and incredibly powerful statement of our commitment to our digital agenda. I just wish I'd done it 12 months ago when I started this process, not just a few weeks ago.

'The second thing I'd do differently is that I'd have automatically or immediately stopped all or most of the work on the "bright and shiny things". These are the initiatives and projects going on around the business when I joined which were something of a distraction. What I mean by that is that people get excited by the bright and shiny things and they lose sight of the fact that actually we need to fix the basics first.

'Customers are not going to join us because we provide banking services through a smart watch or because we offer video banking capability to some of our segments, or whatever it might be. They might be interested in those things, but if we don't get the basics right, if they can't do their routine banking through digital channels and it's not a beautiful, seamless, intuitive, personalized experience, then all of those other things don't really matter.

'Now that's not to say that you shouldn't be doing those things or doing some investigation because obviously in terms of trying to continue to innovate, you need to have some resource and some attention devoted to those things. But don't lose sight of the fact that you need to focus on your core competence first. And again, it comes back to customers. What are customers doing with you at the moment? What is it that they want from you? What is it that they expect from you? And address those issues first. Get those absolutely perfect, and then you can start accelerating all the work around the bright and shiny things.'

Ian Morgan, Managing Director, Digital Channels, Barclays UK

Martin Fewell, The Metropolitan Police

'If I could go back 18 months I'd fight for more time with management colleagues, I'd do more and more varied types of engagement with them.

'I'd get them to spend more time looking at organizations that are successfully digitized, and more time with their customers, the public. And probably the thing that I probably gave up a bit too soon on and was getting a really good reception, was creating really good digital tools they could use to improve their ability to do their job.

'So, like a lot of organizations, we have our daily dashboard of what's going on in the organization. It's pretty analogue, it's not a great tool. It doesn't allow you to self-serve and analyse the data particularly easily, for instance if you wanted to look at what's happening in a particular borough or look at the figures in a different way. We can't do that at the moment.

'I thought that what would really start to open the eyes of the Management Board, is if we could create a really good digital dashboard that they could start to use, to start to influence behaviours and ways of working from the top.

'We've all got work iPads with access to some of our systems and data is another really important aspect of policing, we're constantly obsessing about statistics, crime rates and so on, so it felt like a natural place to start to have that influence. I believe that giving people digital tools to really understand data and analyse it themselves might awaken a broader interest in digital, and stop it being something they feel uncomfortable with. And I think you've got to operate at that personal micro-level, as well as at an organizational transformation level as well.

'It's actually something I've just written down that I'm going to revisit because I really do think it could be a powerful tool.'

Martin Fewell, Director of Media and Communications, The Metropolitan Police | @martinfewell

Simon Thompson, HSBC

'When I was at Morrison's, we presented a revolutionary digital vision to the Board. I still look at it now, the team produced a great piece of thinking, it was a complete reinvention of the supermarket. It's really cool. An all-glass store design with a live customer comment Twitter feed around the roof. The ability to speak to the people making your food in real time, giving the customer the chance to ask for "extra cheese" if they wished. A new delivery experience allowing the customers to fill up with food and fuel in under two minutes – you drove your car in, someone fuelled it, put the food in the back and off you went. You never even had to leave your seat. We were baking hot bread just by the delivery point, so that when you were actually driving home you could enjoy that glorious smell... plus many more super ideas.

'So that's where we started. Where we ended was with a realization that what the the customer actually needed was a delivery of family basics such as milk and fresh food, exactly as they had ordered (no substitutions), perfectly on time (not early or late), with a long "date life" and for the business a model that would make money. We realized that we had to start with the practical realities, the short-term things that we needed to execute at a scale that would actually make a difference right away. This became known as doing the basics brilliantly, and that was a hard thing to do.

'You've always got to keep an eye on the destination. You can't underestimate the power of momentum. The day we got true support for the online business was the day that everyone got a delivery at home. A number of my board colleagues received calls from their partners that day saying "I've just had the most amazing service" and suddenly the light bulbs came on. Online is a good thing, let's support it 100 per cent.

'You can talk as much as you want, but when people see real things they get involved. I remember making many presentations during the launch journey, but when we showed the first website actually working people suddenly said "wow, this is real". PowerPoint doesn't cut it. Only reality counts. 1 out of 10 for the idea. 9 out of 10 for the execution.'

Simon Thompson, Global Head of Digital Commerce, HSBC PLC

Dominic Grounsell, Travelex

'If I had my time again, I would spend a lot more time communicating the context, strategy and agenda for the transformation right across the organization. When you're going through a big change process, there really is no such thing as too much communication.

'We were very ambitious with our product agenda and arguably bit off more than we could chew in the service of driving as much momentum as possible as quickly as possible. It's only when we got things moving that we fully realized how incredibly complicated it would be to build and connect so many new products and technologies all at the same time.

'Engaging and exciting stakeholders at all levels of the business is crucial to the success of any transformation. We initially focused our energy on communicating with leaders and managers and, on reflection, we should have moved earlier to get the whole staff base on board. That may have helped eliminate some of the challenges we experienced in the early days of the transformation.'

Dominic Grounsell, Global Marketing Director, Travelex | @DomGrounsell

Kristof Fahy, Ladbrokes

'I've only been with Ladbrokes for a few months, but if I think back to the transformation I led at William Hill, and could go back in time and re-brief myself, I think the I would have embraced single-customer-view technology platforms sooner.

'To truly transform into digital business, customer metrics have to become business metrics. I think you can only do that if you have a single view of the customer and a really clear, robust, "one customer" platform.

'We spent too long exploring and thinking about this, we weren't decisive enough. And I think that held us back from putting that customer agenda right in the centre of the business quickly enough.

'My second do-over would have been to have pushed harder. I pushed very hard for change but I think I could have pushed harder and quicker, looking back on it. There are some points at which you could make a left or right decision. And sometimes you turn left because it's either politically astute or you don't think you're going to get something over the wall. With the benefit of hindsight, I think I turned left for tactical reasons when I should have just differed and gone with what my gut told me was the right thing to do, even if not the easiest.'

Kristof Fahy, Chief Marketing Officer, Ladbrokes plc | @kpf1970

Caitlin Blewett, Deloitte

'Prior to joining Deloitte, I spent more than a decade working at some of the world's leading creative agencies, marketing everything from commercial and institutional banking to lipstick and luxury ocean liners... very different worlds to that of professional services.

'If I could go back to my first day at Deloitte and give myself a piece of advice, it would be to reiterate something that one of our partners said to me in an introductory meeting, which was, "Challenge us, don't just do things because that's how they've always been done. Keep pushing us forward."

'I've continued to encounter that direction and feedback from across the business, with people saying "Keep bringing us new ideas, even if we say no a million times, don't stop."

'Amidst whatever challenging complexities you might face, you have to keep a hold of your relentless passion, drive and energy to propel the organization forward.'

Caitlin Blewett, Director, Head of Digital, Deloitte UK | @CaiteBlewett

Gordon Nardini, Travelport

'I would like to have had more time for in depth customer research and journey mapping, to gain a more comprehensive understanding what our customers want. I would prefer to have been able to build better validated foundations. I would like to have had the digital team and the strategists in place, and fully bedded down before we started the programme and not tried to run both the digital transformation and recruitment in parallel.

'I'd like to have spoken to more companies that have already experienced this journey and got more of an understanding from them of the potential challenges I would face. I'd also like to have taken more time to have talked to the wider marketing organization about what we were trying to achieve in the initial 6 month window.

'Embarking on a digital transformation can cause distress in an organization because people get concerned about what it means to them and their role. You can teach an old dog new tricks and you can get a leopard to change its spots, I do believe this! Nonetheless, investing time in helping people to understand what it means for them can ease nervousness and pay dividends in the long-run.'

Gordon Nardini, Senior Director, Marketing, Travelport | @flufforfact

Your digital culture audit

The starting point for any sort of change initiative is to look inside your organization and take stock of where you are today. Knowing where you are starting from will help you to identify quick wins, to prioritize where to focus your efforts in the early stages of a transformation, and to highlight strengths as well as weaknesses.

In Part Three of this book, we take you through the Digital Culture Framework, a set of key considerations to help you to build an organizational culture that is attuned to the constantly changing, digital world we live in.

Before you jump into the 'how' which those chapters provide, start by working through this audit to clarify where you think you are today. Each section of this audit contains five statements. Give yourself a score between zero and 10, where zero is 'very strongly disagree' and 10 is 'very strongly agree'. At the end of the audit, add up your scores for each section using the table provided, and you will have a snapshot of your current assessment of your digital culture.

With each section carrying a maximum of 50 points, you will be able to see, for each of the 14 aspects of digital culture, how you stand today on a relative basis. Clearly this is not a scientific process, it is very subjective – but that is the point. Your opinions on each of the statements below are absolutely relevant, because it is you who wants to be part of the efforts to make change happen. What is even more useful, is to ask some carefully selected colleagues to go through this same exercise, as differences in opinion will be useful to stimulate discussion.

Definition and vision

- Our leaders and managers have a clear and shared understanding of how digital technology is impacting our business.

- We have clearly articulated the business need to transform into a truly digital business.
- Everyone in our organization has a shared understanding of what 'being digital' means for our business.
- Leaders and managers understand what digital transformation means for their own parts of the business.
- We have a clearly articulated vision for our digital transformation that has been shared and is understood across our organization.

Leadership

- Our CEO is a key ambassador for digital in our organization, constantly reinforcing our ambitions, getting personally involved and role-modelling our desired ways of working and behaviours.
- Our CEO continually challenges leaders on their commitment to our digital agenda, aligns managers throughout the business and resolves conflicts.
- Building our digital capability is a shared objective owned by all of our leadership team.
- Our digital goals and KPIs are cascaded beyond our leadership team into all of our functions.
- Resources, budgets and plans throughout the organization reflect our digital ambitions and priorities.

Agility

- We are fast-paced and decisive when it comes to new digital initiatives.
- Wherever possible, decision-making on new digital initiatives is delegated to project teams, rather than senior managers.
- We empower project teams by delegating decision-making and remove hierarchies or sign-off delays wherever possible.
- We work on a test-and-learn basis, regularly learning from testing with customers and iterating as needed.
- We are skilled at working in cross-functional teams on digital projects to identify barriers and blockers to progress, and collaborating to resolve them.

Environment

- Our working environment promotes collaboration.
- We used open and co-working spaces to help our people to work across teams and functions to improve pace and speed of working.
- We use our working environment to reinforce our digital vision and update colleagues on progress and performance.
- We use digital technology in the workplace to improve the day-to-day employee working experience.
- We have adapted our working environment to help us attract great digital talent.

Skills and talent

- We have clearly articulated the skills and talent needed in our business to make our digital ambitions a reality.
- We have overhauled our recruitment process to give us access to a wider pool of talent, and to identify the best digital candidates with greater certainty.
- We use a diverse and innovative range of learning approaches beyond the classroom, to appeal to a range of different learning types and take advantages of advances in learning technology.
- Our employees take their learning and development seriously, and work together with management to ensure it is given the time it warrants.
- We encourage experimentation and an environment where failure is not stigmatized, to help learning transfer to the business as soon as possible.

Strategic positioning

- We have a clear and distinctive strategic (or brand) positioning that is universally understood within our business.
- Our strategic positioning goes beyond communications and informs how we design experiences with our business.
- The digital culture we aspire to build is strongly aligned to our strategic positioning.
- Our strategic positioning informs how we design digital user journeys within our business.

- When we create content to engage with our customers, it authentically reflects our core purpose as a business.

Translation and communication

- We tailor our communications about our digital ambitions and digital performance to make it relevant and meaningful to different departments and at different levels.
- We maintain an ongoing commitment to communicating our digital vision and reiterating our change priorities.
- We have a network of digital evangelists in our business who help us to share our work to become a truly digital business.
- We proactively seek out and act on ideas, feedback and constructive criticism on our digital agenda from colleagues throughout the business.
- We use digital technology effectively in our internal communications to help role-model behaviours and ways of working.

Technology

- Our IT team works in close partnership with those leading our digital transformation efforts.
- We have a single view of our customer and ensure all of our systems are integrated.
- Our IT team helps to educate our leaders and the wider business on the implications of our technology choices.
- Technology (systems and infrastructure) decisions are made collaboratively within our business.
- Our IT team is seen as an internal service provider, rather than a department focused on risk mitigation, and internal customer satisfaction is a key measure of its performance.

Process and governance

- We have identified and mapped the key internal processes that impact our digital agenda.
- We use internal service level agreements to ensure interdependencies between teams are understood and work in synch.

- We review and iterate our governance and sign-off processes regularly to ensure they remain fit for purpose.
- Our internal processes are trained into our teams and used consistently, rather than left languishing in a drawer somewhere.
- We use workplace experimentation to test and refine new processes and ways of working to help mitigate risk.

Structure

- Our organization design is optimal for supporting a digital transformation.
- Our internal structure helps our efforts to build digital capability, more than it hinders it.
- The leadership of our digital agenda is optimal for supporting a digital transformation (we have the right role, in the right place in the business).
- Our digital team(s) are well integrated into the business, regardless of how we are structured, and are not perceived as a silo.
- We have a set of routines that ensure information and communication on our digital developments flows around the organization in a timely way, without interruption.

Connections

- We share knowledge and collaborate with other members of our value chain on digital developments.
- We work closely with key customers to inform our digital agenda.
- Our digital people are well networked and proactively seek to build connections with people and businesses that can add value to our digital efforts.
- We create (and protect) time for our people to get out of the business and access learning and information-gathering events.
- We proactively engage with start-ups and the digital community to help educate us on new thinking and developments.

Measurement

- Our core business objectives are clearly articulated in ways which make them measurable and relevant to our digital agenda.

- We can connect the impact of our investment in digital initiatives on primary customer or market objectives.
- Our digital analytics are aligned to clear campaign objectives, which are connected to overarching business goals.
- Our finance team works in partnership with digital, marketing and other teams to improve the measurability of our investments and connect metrics to our primary customer or market objectives.
- We have a single, comprehensive measurement framework that helps us to understand the ROI for each of our channels.

Innovation and entrepreneurship

- We have clear communication from our leaders that positively encourages experimentation and testing.
- We do not stigmatize failure and we proactively share lessons learned from our digital experimentation.
- Market insights are shared widely within our organization to help different teams to identify opportunities for innovation.
- We have clear processes in place to enable and govern experimentation, and to support a culture of managed risk.
- We incentivize and reward individuals and teams for developing new ideas or experiments.

Financial

- We can connect the impact of our investment in digital initiatives on financial outcomes and business performance.
- Our finance team works in partnership with digital, marketing and other teams to improve the measurability of our investments and connect metrics to financial outcomes and business impact.
- We use financial impact assessments as part of developing business cases for investments in new digital initiatives.
- Where financial measurability is not possible, we collaborate effectively to agree alternative, robust performance evaluation.
- Financial impact is not the only criteria we use to evaluate investment in new digital initiatives – it is important, but we take a balanced approach so as not to stifle innovation and experimentation.

Your digital audit scores

You can use Table 6.1 to capture your scores, or download an electronic version from www.targetinternet.com/digitalculture.

Table 6.1 Your digital audit scores

Audit area	Your score	Out of
Definition and vision		50
Leadership		50
Agility		50
Environment		50
Skills and talent		50
Strategic positioning		50
Translation and communication		50
Technology		50
Process and governance		50
Structure		50
Connections		50
Measurement		50
Innovation and entrepreneurship		50
Financial		50

Digital culture audit score summary

As we mentioned at the start of this chapter, this is not designed to be a scientific process. The aim of asking yourself these questions is to take something of a pulse check about how you currently rate your organization's digital culture and capability.

It is most useful, firstly, when you encourage colleagues to go through the same exercise and see what differences in opinion emerge, and to use it as a conversation starter when you are thinking about building your plan to bring about change in your business. Secondly, it is something that you can revisit in 12 months' time and to see where you have or have not made the progress you were hoping for.

Understanding your stakeholders 07

Bringing about change in any organization – whether a small domestic operator, or a complex multinational enterprise – is not something you can do alone. Sure, you need a passionate, determined and resilient individual to lead your digital agenda, and ideally a small team of change agents to work with and on your behalf. But you also need to corral support, commitment and action from a range of others in the business, and not just those at the top of the organization.

Different people will react to your agenda in different ways. Some will be immediately supportive, some will be quietly sceptical, others will not show an interest, and others may actively work to disrupt your plans. A number of different factors influence whether or not you will secure the support you need from a given stakeholder – the key is to be proactive in identifying these, making sure you are on the front foot and prepared for any outcome.

Mapping your stakeholders

In reality, not all stakeholders are created equal. It is a little like targeting customer segments – some represent greater value than others.

There is little point in spending copious amounts of time in discussions with an individual who, despite his or her interest or enthusiasm for your agenda, can make little difference to the success of your outcome. That may sound a little blunt, but in a world of finite time and resource, you cannot afford to underinvest your time with a stakeholder whose support may make or break your plans.

There are several ways you can map your stakeholders, using a simple and flexible 2×2 matrix. The first is *power and interest* (Mendelow, 1991). This involves considering how interested stakeholders are likely to be in your project, against how much influence or power they have to help you to get things done.

The second is *importance and influence*. Here, you consider how important stakeholders are to the success of your project, against how much influence or power they have to help you to get things done.

The third is *impact and influence*. Here, you consider how much impact your digital agenda will have on different stakeholders, against how much influence or power they have to help you to get things done.

The great thing about a 2×2 matrix is that you can change the dimensions to suit your specific needs or context. You can also use it in a light-touch way, based on your opinions or discussion with others to help 'plot' different departments or individuals. Alternatively, you can use it with a little more structure, asking a common set of questions, then scoring different departments or individuals in order to plot them based on more than just a hunch. Let's explore the use of the impact and influence matrix.

Impact and influence matrix

To use this tool in practice, start with a clear definition of impact and influence, and develop some questions you can use to determine how best to score and plot your key stakeholders (Figure 7.1 – you can adapt these for your business, they are just an example).

Figure 7.1 Impact and influence matrix

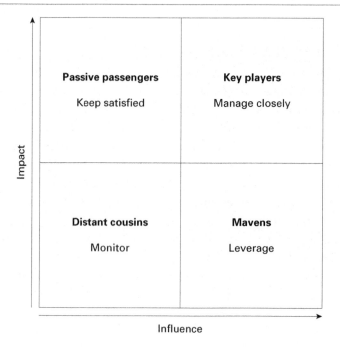

Stakeholder matrix

Definition of impact: Put simply, how much your digital agenda could potentially personally impact individuals or their teams. You might use the following questions to develop a score for each stakeholder – these are written with individuals in mind, but you could just as easily adapt it for departments or teams:

1 Will our digital agenda create vulnerability to this individual's role, or any of his or her team(s)?

2 Will it result in material changes to how this person works or the projects he or she is involved in?

3 Will our agenda affect his or her budgets, either positively or negatively?

4 Will this person be responsible for delivering any aspects of our digital ambitions that he or she is not currently delivering?

5 Will our transformation in any way affect the status or perceived importance of this individual's role in our business?

Definition of influence: the power that stakeholders have over your project. Their ability to influence decisions, support implementation, derail your plans, or influence other people within the business to do any of the same. You might use the following questions to develop a score for each stakeholder – these are written with individuals in mind, but you could just as easily adapt it for departments or teams:

1 Can this individual in any way block decisions or derail our agenda?

2 Is this individual's opinion and sign of support respected by others?

3 Does this individual control key resources, such as people or budgets, that we will need access to?

4 Do we need this individual to support any aspect of our implementation?

5 Will we need this person's input or expertise in any way?

Score each stakeholder you have in mind from zero to five on your questions such as those above, then use the totals to plot them on the corresponding axis.

It can be useful to do this as a discussion exercise with colleagues, or to do it independently and then compare views before reaching a decision and planning how best to secure support and buy-in.

Quick tip

Stakeholder analysis is a useful exercise and can help aid collaboration and communication in meaningful ways. Be careful, however, not to share your 2×2 matrix (or any of the background questions or scores) with someone whose name features in it, unless you are absolutely sure he or she will be comfortable with it.

People can react negatively to the idea of being analysed and judged, and may not respond well to seeing your assessments of their influence within your business or your determination of how important they really are (or are not) to your project.

Different approaches for different stakeholders

As the matrix shows, the four grids in which you will plot individuals or teams are different, both in the role that stakeholders will play in your digital transformation, and the approach you will take to engaging with them:

- *Key players*. This group is an important priority. Your digital agenda will have a high impact on key players' roles, and they have the influence within the business to either support or negatively impact it. You will want to work closely with them, and manage them closely to ensure they remain aligned to your agenda.

- *Passive passengers*. This group is a moderate priority. Your digital agenda will have a high impact on passive passengers' roles, but they lack the influence to change or significantly impact your chosen direction. You will want to keep them satisfied so that they do not become a disruptive force over time.

- *Mavens*. This group is a moderate priority. Your agenda will not have much impact on mavens personally so their needs will be low, but they are influential within the business so they can be leveraged as supporters on the sidelines, or engaged to help you to engage or influence others.

- *Distant cousins*. This group is a low priority. Your agenda has a low impact on distant cousins, and they cannot do much to influence it anyway. In the spirit of openness and building the right sort of culture, you will want to keep them informed, but from a distance with limited resource impact for you.

Plan your dialogue

Once you have mapped your stakeholder landscape, you can start planning how you will communicate with, and manage your stakeholders. Use the questions below as a guide to help you to identify the best way to engage with people in the most effective way.

You may not think it is necessary to prepare so much for every stakeholder, so you can make your planning lighter-touch for some if it feels more straightforward. Do not underestimate how useful this can be, though. Depending on how much change you are potentially trying to bring about, investing a little time in planning your stakeholder engagement up front can pay dividends further down the line, avoiding conflicts which can cause delays or set you back a few steps.

- What is the context for each stakeholder?
- Who do you need to see first?
- What are your objectives for each stakeholder?
- What is your core messaging?
- What is your stakeholder's likely response to your digital agenda?
- What potential objections might you face and how will you tackle them?
- What channels/communication approaches are best?
- How regular does your engagement need to be?
- What will your stakeholder need from you?

Your strategic approach 08

The problem with the word 'transformation', is that it can be a bit daunting, at the best of times. By its very definition it implies large-scale change, which can immediately raise concerns among some about risk, cost, resource and the capacity to embark on a major change initiative while also trying to run the business today.

In reality, while the end-goal may well be a marked change to your organization's digital capability and its culture, the journey to get there does not have to be quite so daunting. There are several different ways to approach a transformation, and it does not have to involve 'boiling the ocean'.

> Once you have a sense of direction, start to talk about it internally, and find partners and supporters. Start small and try and get some quick wins. Don't boil the ocean from day one. Show you can implement at a grass roots level.
> *Russ Shaw, Founder, Tech London Advocates | @RussShaw1*

Choosing a path

There are several strategic approaches that can be used to get traction, depending on the level of commitment and resources within your organization. These include:

- test cases;
- planned incrementalism;
- strategy by stealth;
- major change.

We will explore each of these in this chapter, looking at what each approach involves, the resources you need and their pros and cons, in order to help you to identify which might be best for you.

Test cases

A test-case approach to a digital transformation involves starting small and developing what is often referred to in marketing and product development as a 'proof of concept'.

Here, rather than seeking commitment to a large-scale programme of change and investment, potentially of two or three years, you focus on proving that a different approach to leveraging digital technology for the benefit of your business can yield dividends, before seeking commitment to a bigger or more ambitious set of initiatives.

This approach is particularly useful if your organization is particularly risk-averse, has suffered from failed projects and change programmes in the recent past, or had its fingers burned with investments in digital technology that have not delivered on their promises. It can also be helpful if you want to prove that your business has the capability to manage change and deliver on its commitments.

Pros

The advantage of this approach is that you will be able to start your digital transformation in a manageable, tightly defined and controlled way. By focusing on one initiative to develop your test case, for instance digitizing a key customer process or introducing a new digital way of working in your customer support team, you will be dealing with less stakeholder complexity and have greater control over the project and its various moving parts. On completion, you will have a stronger story to sell-in to your top team to help make the case for pursuing a bigger, more ambitious agenda.

Cons

There are two main downsides to this approach. Firstly, it ups the stakes. You have got to be certain you are choosing the best project as a test case, one without significant stakeholder complexity or conflict. Also, make sure that you are not choosing something with significant technology dependencies as that may inhibit your ability to deliver if wider investment is needed to support it. The second downside to this approach is that you risk having your test case strung along to a second, then a third, then a fourth, without securing the organization's commitment to the more substantial transformation that you need. This will ultimately limit your effectiveness, as ad hoc projects can only get you so far before you need to make some bigger investments or commitments, for instance in technology platforms or systems such as marketing automation, CRM or web platform. It will also restrict your ability to bring about sustained cultural change.

Planned incrementalism

This approach involves a carefully managed approach to a digital transformation. It involves securing buy-in from your leadership team to your longer-term digital ambitions, but committing to start on smaller-scale, more foundational projects.

Rather than taking the cost or the risk of big, transformative projects too early on, it emphasizes a more conservative, incremental, 'small steps' approach. This is particularly helpful if your organization has resource constraints (either in terms of people's capacity or capability, or in terms of financial resources ie capital expenditure).

It can enable you to work towards a longer-term ambition but in the early stages (ie years one and two), getting the basics right, making an impact on business performance and building capital for investments in bigger bets and innovations further down the line.

Pros

This approach is fundamentally pragmatic, so for certain types of business it will ensure that your vision for digital transformation is not seen as a pipe dream, or too detached from the realities and constraints your business faces.

Cons

The risk with this approach is that you are outmanoeuvred or outpaced by faster-moving competitors, or disruptors not yet known to your industry. In addition, you may find it difficult to maintain support for bigger future investments or innovations, as over time the business (and its leaders) settle into a comfort zone where change around the fringes is working all right, and broadly speaking the business is performing well, raising questions as to whether more risky change is actually necessary? You risk losing your 'burning platform' for change.

Strategy by stealth

Strategy by stealth is a risky approach, but one which can pay dividends (if you are willing to take the chance). It involves either acknowledging that top-team buy-in to your digital ambitions is unlikely, or for some reason not desirable (such as a lack of access to or engagement with your senior leaders).

This approach involves articulating your digital ambitions and corralling a small group of colleagues who support the ambition, to attempt to make change happen under the radar. This means avoiding any form of leadership engagement or internal communication of a digital vision, and instead working 'off book' to start to make early progress without the endorsement or buy-in of leaders.

At this point, you may be asking why we would advocate such an approach. Surely it flies in the face of pretty much everything else in this book? Well, you would be right. We are not advocating or endorsing this approach, but for some businesses it may be their only realistic choice and one which has been known to be used effectively.

You see, for some people (and granted, a minority – we hope!), there is simply not enough awareness or understanding of the impact of digital technology within their business. No amount of storytelling, impassioned presentations or statistics will convince leaders to accept anything but the status quo. The only thing that this top team might face up to is cold, hard proof from their own business, even if they did not sanction it.

Ultimately, this is a short-lived approach, and one which is more prepara-tory than conclusive. The aim is to get as far as possible with introducing digital change to your business to be able to put irrefutable evidence in front of decision makers, that they have to change, that the change is real, and it is already underway.

Pros

This is naturally somewhat limited. The benefits of this approach are limited, but for those facing no other alternative (short of considering alternative employment), it may be the only option available to force the change agenda. If it works, you may finally have the catalyst you need to get digital firmly on the management team's agenda, and then pursue an alternative approach from this selection.

Cons

This is naturally somewhat more significant. The risks to this approach are not to be underestimated. At the very least, you may end up diverting time and budget to endeavours which do not yield an impact on 'business as usual', leading to questions about judgement. At the other extreme, no matter how right you may be, leaders may take a very dim view of off-book, even underhand operations, which could lead to your original alternative options of seeking employment elsewhere.

Major change

At the other end of the extreme, an all-in approach does what it says on the tin. Here, you have managed to secure commitment to a far-reaching programme of change and your leadership team has bitten the bullet and signed up to it.

An all-in approach is the most ambitious route to digitally transform your organization. It is well suited to businesses that have access to financial resource and talent that enables them to take an accelerated approach to building digital capability. It is demanding, and the stakes are high, but for those who succeed, it can bring about change in a more profound way than other approaches.

You will not only need strong digital leadership, digital talent and access to capital to make the investments needed. You will also need deep expertise in stakeholder engagement, internal communication and change management, among other things we discuss in more detail in Part Three of this book.

Taking an all-in approach does not necessarily mean skirting over the fundamentals or only jumping into the big bets and big innovations. Building test cases and pursuing incremental improvements, as discussed earlier in this chapter, can still apply with an all-in approach to digital transformation. The difference is that you have secured a mandate for wide-reaching change, and your organization is willing to signal to both employees, customers and wider stakeholders that it is serious about its role in the new digital world order.

Pros

Doubling-down on digital transformation gives you the best possible chance of staying ahead of competitors, preparing for future disruptions, and enacting meaningful culture change within your business. A mandate to take the necessary steps to overhaul the culture and practices of a business to position it for success in a constantly changing world lends an authenticity to your internal communication and engagement efforts and can help overcome resistance below the upper ranks of an organization.

Cons

Major change programmes raise the stakes. All-in also means all-or-nothing. Incremental success of an agenda that promised more radical change will potentially be viewed dimly, irrespective of the progress it has made. It also increases the scale and complexity of the challenge ahead. If an organization's leadership team commits people, budget and other resources to a series of significant digital initiatives, those leading them may find themselves subject to conflicting or overwhelming demands from internal stakeholders to 'prioritize their part of the business first'.

No silver bullet

There is no single way of building digital capability and positioning your organization for success in a digital world. Each approach outlined above has its merits and its shortfalls, the key is to understand which best suits the context facing your business.

The purpose of describing each of these approaches is also to reassure you (and help you to reassure colleagues) that it is not a case of 'bet the farm or nothing'. Progress can be made in different ways and your approach can evolve over time. If you begin with test cases, you can progress to planned incrementalism. If you start with planned incrementalism, you can step up a gear to an all-in approach.

Your approach to digital transformation can – and likely will – evolve over time. You will learn from your early successes and missteps. The environment you are operating will evolve over time and competitor activity may present an opportunity (or force you) to adapt your plans. That is a reality of this constantly changing environment we are operating in. Adaptability is key, but so is having a sense of direction to start with.

CASE STUDY   Deloitte's digital transformation journey

In 2015, Deloitte UK began to lay the foundations for a three-year digital journey, designed to fundamentally overhaul how the 'big four' professional services firm harnessed the power of digital to engage with, and develop prominence among, clients both of today and tomorrow. Caitlin Blewett, Director and Head of Digital at Deloitte UK, explains in this guest article.

Prior to 2015, we had a range of disparate 'digital' teams and discipline experts. There was a content team, a technology team, a user experience team and so on. While each of these teams were 'digital' in focus – they existed in silos.

In some instances, they were working in tune, but in other instances they were focused on different priorities and varied initiatives that didn't necessarily add up to a bigger strategic picture.

So the change, and the creation of my role, was to define a digital strategy and vision to evolve our digital presence, along the way understanding what each of the existing 'digital' areas were focused on and where changes needed to be made.

Today, we have one digital team working to execute one digital strategy. Of course within the overarching strategy, there are specific priorities for individual disciplines, but they're part of the same bigger picture.

Developing a plan

I have a Thomas Edison quote on my wall – 'Vision without execution is just a hallucination' – which is a constant reminder that while defining an ambitious vision and strategy are critical, it is equally important to ensure that you are clear about how you will move forward.

To do this, we've designed a three-year road map, not in the traditional sense of saying 'we've written a plan, don't worry, it'll all be great'. Rather, we've created a practical framework that helps us to pursue the right things, at the right time.

There are two basic components to this framework.

The first component focuses on the establishment of the *key digital disciplines* in which we need to build our capability. For Deloitte, we have defined six disciplines to focus further developing our capabilities in; data and analytics, marketing automation, social media, content marketing, campaigns and platforms and technology.

The second component focuses on how we will develop and progress each discipline, moving through *various stages of maturity* over the three-year period.

Year one

The first phase of our roadmap is all about brilliant basics. This, as the name suggests, is about doing the fundamentals really, really well, without getting distracted by the art of the possible or stakeholder demands.

It's possibly one of the most important parts of our journey, and the most challenging to stay true to. You have to continue to stress to stakeholders that first and foremost ensuring the solid foundations are in place is critical and manage expectations accordingly.

When you embark on an exciting digital endeavour, demands are high because there's so much you could do, but there's little point in doing so if you haven't got the basics in place. For instance, building a really cool app when your core website isn't fully optimized, or embarking on clever social media campaigns when you don't have a social channel strategy in place.

These basics aren't necessarily the sexy or cool aspects of digital that people expect to see in a transformation initiative, but they are nonetheless critical. Technical SEO audits, canonical linking, basic website user experience functionality and so on. It may not be glamorous but it's an important foundation for any brand that exists today, and building on shaky foundations is never a good idea.

I'm really happy for us to experiment with new and innovative ideas, but experimentation must be done in conjunction with things working properly. So year one is all about nailing the brilliant basics.

Year two

Year two will focus on driving differentiation. Once we have the basics in place, we build on them to genuinely set ourselves apart among a very similar set of competitors. For many businesses, if you take away logos and branding, the core products and services which businesses provide are much of the same… it's difficult to differentiate at a product or service level. Where differentiation really comes into play is *how* you engage your clients through distinctive marketing and differentiated experiences.

Year three

Third year focus is on ensuring we are future-fit. This is where we'll be pursuing much more forward-looking and innovative digital initiatives, but whatever they are, they'll be looking towards the future and build on our brilliant basics and strides made in driving differentiated experiences.

Phased with flexibility

The aim of the roadmap is to give ourselves a structure that helps us to plan and prioritize, and makes sense to stakeholders. It helps us to explain what we're doing and why, and gives our teams a common framework. In each of our six core digital disciplines, there's a plan for brilliant basics, a plan for differentiation, and a plan for being future-fit.

However, it is important to note that while we talk about year one, two and three, we're not saying that everything has to happen linearly, things can and should happen in parallel, such as working on concepts for being future-fit in some areas, even though we're in the brilliant basics phase.

Ultimately, this framework is invaluable because it's used for multiple purposes from securing buy-in, to planning our efforts, tracking our progress as a team, and communicating more widely within the business. It also helps to demystify and make practical the complex notion of 'digital'.

PART THREE
The Digital Culture Framework

This Part gives you a structured framework of all of the things you will need to consider to build an organization that is operating in a constantly changing environment. The Part works as both a checklist, but also as a reference and guide that you revisit as you take on the particular challenges involved.

READINESS

Strategic positioning
Translation and communication
Technology
Process and governance
Structure
Connections

ESSENTIALS

Definition and vision
Leadership
Agility
Environment
Skills and talent

PERFORMANCE

Measurement
Innovation and entrepreneurship
Financial

DIGITAL CULTURE

Definition and vision

Lots of people talk about 'being digital', but do we know what that actually means? Around 10–15 years ago, being digital meant having a website, but today it has evolved to mean something much broader and more complex; as digital technologies have become more pervasive in our everyday lives, so too have they in our organizations.

> I think we've gone from an era of digital infancy to an era of semi-maturity, or 'digital adolescence'. Whereas before digital was this exciting experimental frontier, it's now no longer about dipping a toe in the water or trying something. It can mean life or death in business for a brand, particularly if your competition is more adept, digitized and future-focused in their outlook than you are.
> *Joe Petyan, Executive Partner, J Walter Thompson London*

For some people, digital is still primarily about marketing communications. Some think it is about technology, while for others it is about apps. These views are not necessarily wrong, but for most organizations, the challenge is that there is no *consistent* understanding of what being digital means, and that can quickly lead to wasted resources, conflicting priorities and missed opportunities.

A critical ingredient in building a digital culture and succeeding with efforts to transform an organization, is to agree what being digital means (and just as importantly, what it does not mean) for your organization, and then painting a clear picture of this vision for your whole organization.

> So we're not particularly digital, and that's a challenge. Historically, our leaders have tended to see digital transformation as being about better IT. So, our investments and efforts have been very focused on new kit and the IT department delivering it. Giving the tools to people in the front line so they can do their job better, which is probably the way all organizations thought, maybe, 10–15 years ago. The difference for me today lies in not asking 'how can we use this kit to do our jobs more effectively?', but instead asking 'how does digital change the way in which we do our jobs completely?' *Martin Fewell, Director of Media and Communications, The Metropolitan Police | @martinfewell*

Listening first

One of my favourite sayings is 'you have two ears and one mouth for a reason – listen before you speak!' This is particularly important when it comes to defining digital for your business, because it has become so pervasive – no part of an organization is immune to its impact.

Whether you are a newly appointed Head of Digital charged with leading a digital transformation, or you are trying to build a case for making digital a higher priority within your business, start by getting out and asking some pertinent questions.

It is essential to get input from all – or as many as feasible – of your organization's leadership team, as they will be the group you ultimately need to approve and support any changes to make your digital transformation happen. But, in larger organizations in particular, it is especially important to go further into the business and talk to department heads and frontline teams who are closer to operational realities and the customer.

Getting the pulse: key questions

Once you have identified whom it would be helpful to talk to, arrange 10–15 minutes with each of them and ask them the following six questions:

- What does the word 'digital' mean to you?
- What do you think 'being digital' means for our business?
- Where do you think digital technology is going to have most impact on our business in the future?
- On a scale of 1–10, how would you rate our digital capability as a business and why?
- Where do you think the immediate opportunities are for digital to improve our customers' experience of our organization?
- What do you think is our biggest weakness when it comes to digital?

Some people you talk to may not be sure of the right answers, and most of them will give you different views, but that is the point. Taking a little time to ask the right questions internally, before you have even started thinking about strategy, will ensure you know where you are starting from. It will help you to understand the extent to which key people in your organization have shared views about what being digital means, the priorities for your business, and where there are clear differences in opinion.

This exercise will also be educational for you. No single individual can hope to fully understand every corner of the organization, every business process, and every customer interaction. By talking to leaders and managers across the organization and experts from around the business, you will be able to glean insights and ideas which may otherwise have been overlooked.

> The best piece of advice is probably, just listen to people. When I joined City AM I spent my first two weeks just listening. Meeting with people all around the organization, and hearing what they had to say about our digital priorities and agenda, and almost not opening my mouth – even though I desperately wanted to. *Charles Yardley, Chief Operating Officer, City AM*

Having these conversations will give you clarity, and the take-outs from the exercise will be useful in several ways. Firstly, you will be in a position to play back to senior decision makers just how diverse (or inconsistent) the organization's grasp of digital is. Secondly, it will help identify the gap in understanding of what people *think* being digital means, versus what it *actually* means (we discuss the latter further on in this chapter). Thirdly, it will help you to identify existing digital initiatives or projects which might have an impact on your customer experience. Lastly, it will ensure that any efforts to bring about a transformation within your organization start on the right footing: an organization-wide view, in an open and consultative manner.

> I think it's always important, before kicking off any project, to understand the needs and opinions of the key stakeholders in your business. This isn't about finding out how to keep people happy, it's about understanding the context for them and their part of the business, and what change might look like. Starting with this context will enable you to make your project relevant to individual stakeholders, as well as their teams. The easiest way to lose buy-in is to leave people feeling uninvolved or out of the loop. If people feel a sense of involvement in your project, and you've shown that you've listened to them, you're more likely to get their ongoing support. I also think, and I know this is often said (but perhaps less often done), is that it's important to get rid of jargon and buzzwords. You don't need to anchor everything in technical-speak. Try instead saying "By the way, there's a way for us to do this at scale and measure it and prove success". It's about simplifying things for people. Making things unnecessarily difficult or complex makes people less engaged immediately. Listen to them, make it relevant. *Dara Nasr, Managing Director, Twitter UK | @DaraNasr*

> ### 35 interviews, 35 different answers
>
> When Caitlin Blewett, Director and Head of Digital at Deloitte UK, joined the organization in July 2015, she began by trying to get clarity on what 'digital' meant among the professional services firm's leaders.
>
> 'One of the first things I did was interview about 35 Partners and Directors within the business. Across those 35 people, there was a collective of 403 years' experience within Deloitte, so a wealth of organizational and client knowledge. One of the questions I asked all 35 interviewees was, "What is your interpretation of digital?". I did not get the same answer twice.'
>
> What this experience showed Caitlin very quickly was the pressing need to demystify and more clearly articulate the 'digital', giving the word a clear definition and meaning within companies and organizations.
>
> 'The key thing I had to focus on was tackling the buzzwords. Some people thought digital was about the channel, some thought it was technology, some people think it's robots and some think it's about big transformation. We put our energy into dispelling this confusion and really starting to give the word digital some meaning and some context within such a diverse organization. And then doing so consistently, at every opportunity.'

Connecting potential and priority

Thanks to the pace and scale of change in recent years, the possibilities for organizations to harness digital technologies to improve their performance are almost endless. And even as we write this book, new ideas and developments are still being imagined.

In reality, you cannot do everything. To make best use of finite resources, businesses need to apply a filter to all of the things which 'being digital' *could* offer, and find those which are of most pressing priority for them. It may sound obvious, but it is too easy to get caught up in doing the wrong thing for the right reason, or vice versa. It is also important to avoid what we call 'magpie syndrome', where people are drawn to or distracted by what is new and in vogue, often for no reason other than it being possible. This often leads to businesses getting ahead of themselves and missing some of the basics, for instance by developing a cool new app when they have not yet fixed the basics of their web experience.

Organizations on a quest to improve their digital capability and performance often have very different starting points. For some, it may originate with a crisis, such as defecting customers or a disruptive competitor. For others, it may be an opportunity to reduce costs or improve service times. Some organizations try to improve their digital capability incrementally or on an ad hoc basis, while others take a more strategic, larger-scale approach. In many cases, these such efforts may sit only in one team or department, rather than be organization-wide.

It is therefore essential to be clear about what digital priorities your business needs to pursue, in what order, and – most importantly – to take an organization-wide view. This will ensure you are making the most of the resources at hand, are aligning your efforts with business strategy and objectives, and are best placed to ensure your leadership team (and by association, the whole business) are aligned.

Three types of transformation

So you are trying to get your organization to stop acting digital, and start being digital. You are anticipating a number of changes needed across the business and you therefore need to build a digital culture to ensure those changes are embraced, and that they stick.

The trouble is, there is no one 'version' of a transformation to become truly digital. There is not one single blueprint you can follow to become the Google of your sector, as people often phrase it. As you try to connect your priorities with the potential that digital presents, it is important to recognize that transformation manifests itself in three core ways:

- new propositions and business models;
- operational improvement;
- customer experience optimization.

New propositions and business models

Digital technologies have opened up new ways of doing business that only 10 years ago would not have been thought possible, and in some cases even ridiculed.

Step back in time to January 2007. Imagine if someone told you that you would soon use an application on your iPhone (which was still five months away from launch, at that point) to book a taxi, track it as it travels to you, and not need cash to pay as it automatically charges your credit card and sends you a receipt without you needing to be in the car (Uber).

Or if they said you would plan your next holiday by choosing someone else's room or home to stay in anywhere in the world, whom you had never met (Airbnb). Or that your phone would monitor your driving style to ensure you get the best possible insurance premiums. Or that you would use a watch to pay for coffee or to get on the tube, and that your car or phone would track how close you are to home and turn the lights and heating on for you in preparation.

Few of us beyond tech visionaries such as Jobs, Zuckerberg, Brin or Page might have believed these predictions, but today, just 10 short years later, these developments have become 'normal', to the extent many of us would struggle to imagine life without them.

Think of this type of transformation – new propositions and business models – as using digital technology to:

- access customers previously out of reach;
- serve customers in a fundamentally different way;
- change how customers use your product or service;
- build fundamentally new products or services;
- protect or prepare a business from future category or sector disruption.

Operational improvement

Digital technology offers significant potential for improving the efficiency of many internal processes and ways of working, and the motivations behind this sort of transformation are principally for the benefit of your business, rather than the customers' experience (although benefits can be mutual).

We have all experienced some of the outcomes of this sort of digital change. Consider how paperless billing for your utilities and credit card statements has reduced the cost of printing and postage for companies, or how live web-based chats with, say, your mobile provider has reduced the need for telephone customer service agents who can only handle one call at a time, by using virtual customer service advisors who can handle more than one query concurrently.

Operational improvements do not always reach the customer directly. They can also be applied internally to 'back office' or operational activities, which the customer has no exposure to. Consider for instance:

- How inefficient internal management reporting often is, with often lengthy lags between data being available and it reaching those who need to act on it.

- The time it takes to move from preparing a job description to sign-off for external recruitment, to receiving CVs for review and scheduling interviews.
- How progressing a commercial contract through procurement, compliance, finance, legal, risk and other departments remains so reliant on paper copies, internal mail and lengthy processing times.

Ask yourself how digital technology could help make your organization run smoother and slicker, reducing time, errors and costs. Think of this type of transformation – operational improvements – as using digital technology to:

- reduce the time of different parts of a customer transaction/relationship;
- reduce the cost of different parts of a customer transaction/relationship;
- speed up internal processes to aid with faster decision-making and approvals;
- create more transparency around internal processes and data.

Customer experience optimization

The final form in which the transformation to becoming truly digital manifests itself is in connecting, integrating and optimizing the experience your customers have of your brand.

In the early 2000s, as businesses began to invest increasingly in digital marketing channels and activities, customer journeys became increasingly fragmented and inconsistent. During this time, while digital was very much in its infancy, businesses were focused on experimenting with new and unproven tools and techniques, and responding to changing customer behaviours. Consequently, most digital efforts were at a disconnect from 'traditional' or 'analogue' parts of the customer journey.

Most of us can recall a frustrating encounter with a business where dealing with different channels felt like dealing with a different company (the website versus the store versus the call centre). It could feel like a brand was ignoring the data it held on us, for instance your bank offering you a credit card when they should already know you have an existing card with them.

Despite the progress made since the heady days of the early 2000s, many organizations still struggle to connect their customer experience and deliver a consistent and intentional experience across channels. Today, confronted with an ever-increasing set of options to engage with customers, many businesses invest in digital channels because they think they should, but without really understanding whether it is creating value for the customer, and it is this central issue that this type of transformation sets out to tackle.

Think of this type of transformation – customer experience optimization – as using digital technology to:

- make customers' lives easier for them;
- deliver meaningful, relevant content and engagements with customers when, where and how they want it;
- helping customers to transact with or talk to a business on their terms;
- increasing the level of personalization between a business and its customers;
- reducing unnecessary complications in a customer journey;
- seeking out brand differentiation.

'We had a large number of different customer segments, a large number of different product types, and a historically very siloed approach to building our digital platforms for them.

'So we would develop a customer experience for a wealth customer, or we would develop a customer experience for a mortgage customer or for a loan customer. But we weren't really taking that holistic view of what the overarching customer experience should be. It became very siloed, and as a result of that, we've ended up with sub-optimal journeys, a very fragmented experience, a plethora of different websites, a multitude of microsites and a multitude of apps because we've taken this siloed approach to what digital means to each of those segments and each of those product owners.

'So that's one of my main challenges: how do we break down those silos and take a more holistic, horizontal view of how we deliver customer service excellence to our customers via digital channels?'

Ian Morgan, Managing Director, Digital Channels, Barclays UK

What sort of change is right for you?

It is not simply a case of choosing one of these options over another. Rather, this is a helpful way of thinking about change to identify what 'being digital' really means for your business, and where the biggest opportunities and priorities lie.

You should already be armed with some insight from the conversations you have been able to have internally with other stakeholders – you can now build on this by starting to ask some questions against each of these three types of digital transformation.

New propositions and business models

Think about your core products and services, and the established ways in which you deliver them to customers, and ask yourself the following:

- What aspect of our core products and business model is least impacted by digital technology today, and how might this change?
- Who is doing better than us in our market by leveraging technology, and how?
- Who is not in our industry today but is on the periphery, and could move into our space in the future?
- Are we clear enough on our core purpose as an organization or are we being myopic, and could this limit our growth options?
- How could our industry be disrupted, or how could we disrupt it? Are there any adjacent markets or industries which we could use our capability to disrupt?

Operational improvement

Think about the key things that have to happen behind the scenes in order for you to win with customers and meet their expectations, and ask yourself the following:

- What do we think is the slickest part of our behind-the-scenes operation, and why?
- What aspects of our customer engagements take the most time to deliver, and how could we speed these up?
- What aspects of servicing customers requires the most resource (people and financial), and could technology help us reduce costs?
- Where do we have most cross-functional involvement in delivering a customer transaction or experience, and is this working smoothly?
- What are our key competitors doing differently in how they use technology to run their operations behind the scenes, and what can we learn from this?

Customer experience optimization

Think about your customer experience and key customer journeys, pre-sale, during sale, and post-sale, and ask yourself the following:

- How are our customers using digital technology to interact with us, and are we helping them to do so or playing catch up?
- Where are the make or break moments in our customer experience – where are our biggest sources of value creation and differentiation, or value erosion?
- Where does digital currently play a role in our customer experience and our customers' journeys with us?
- What steps in our customer journey(s) are most frustrating for our customers?
- Where is there opportunity to innovate ahead of key competitors in our customer experience, and how might this create value for our customers?

Articulating your vision

As is often paraphrased from Lewis Carroll's *Alice in Wonderland*, 'if you don't know where you're going, any road will take you there'.

Those who help define your organization's desired journey to becoming a truly digital business should, by association, understand and embrace it. But it cannot just live there. For any change journey to be successful, you need to paint a picture of what success looks like for the whole organization, and in terms that will have meaning for them (and we talk in more detail about the importance of translation in Chapter 15).

The focus of this chapter has been about defining what being digital means for your business, firstly by understanding the views and priorities of your leaders and then by exploring where digital technology can make most positive impact on your business, and what your change priorities might be.

The aim is to articulate a single, coherent definition and vision for 'being digital', and then time needs to be invested in selling that story to key stakeholders within the business, to demystify digital and give it meaning and context – especially in large or diverse organizations.

Key characteristics for your digital vision

This is not about crafting yet another collection of corporate buzzwords that means little in the day-to-day running of the business – most organizations have enough of those. It is about creating something akin to a 'north star' for your digital efforts and investments that everyone can understand and use to guide their decisions, not just at a strategic level, but also at an operational one.

In our experience, effective digital visions share several common characteristics – ensure you use these when articulating yours:

1 They are simple and straightforward.
2 They avoid heavy use of jargon or complex language.
3 They start with the ambition, what you are trying to do or achieve.
4 They have a clear outcome, based on how doing this will help your customers.
5 They show the business benefit, how doing this will produce a positive outcome for your organization.
6 They are meaningful to the whole organization, not just one department or channel.
7 They are as clear on what you will not do, as on what you will do.

Digital is probably the number one word that gets misused or misinterpreted in businesses today – you can still have people ask you if you can fix their laptop or Microsoft Windows. In the start of the digital transformation journey in any organization, it's critical to develop a clear vision alongside a few clear KPIs and a simple strategic framework. What is most important for digital leaders is to create a scope framework, something which clearly articulates what is in scope for the digital programme, but, most importantly, what is not. This gives the best opportunity to stay focused and be able to achieve the commercial vision. I think that's vitally important, otherwise you'll end up being pulled in every direction as digital today is just too broad. As people say – it's not digital marketing, it's marketing in a digital world! *Adam Stewart, Global Digital Director, RB plc | @adster1*

Key points

- The word digital means too many things to too many people. It is essential to start any digital change initiative by reaching a shared understanding of what 'being digital' means for your organization.
- Start by listening first. Talk to your organization's leaders as well as departmental experts to understand the digital pulse of the organization. Understand what digital means to them and get their views on your organization's digital strengths, weaknesses and priorities.
- Articulate a digital vision for your business that is simple, jargon-free, meaningful across the business, and includes your ambition as well as benefits for both the customer and your business.

Leadership 10

There's no escaping it. Leadership is an *essential* ingredient in any change endeavour or cultural transformation. Period. With engaged, committed and aligned leaders, you stand a chance of success. Without, you face the guarantee of failure.

This is not a chapter on 'buy-in' or 'getting the board on board'. These terms hardly scratch the surface of what is needed at a leadership level to build a digital culture and make your transformation a success. They both wholly underestimate the task at hand.

To truly become digital your business will need to confront some difficult choices. It will face trade-offs, conflicting priorities, significantly new ways of working, the need to take risks, the need to move out of its comfort zone, and many other moments where decisive and united leadership is a prerequisite.

While the importance of this subject cannot be emphasized enough, we are not just going to focus on the risks of getting this wrong, but the reward for getting it right. Remember, the collective impact of your organization's CEO and leadership team can supercharge your efforts to make cultural change and digital transformation a reality.

I think you need people who are senior enough and therefore empowered enough to set the right working environment. In the case of banks, for instance, they're never not going to have regulations and compliance, and other hurdles that they need to get over. That's always going to be there, that's never going to go away. But instead of the foot soldiers rolling their eyes in dismay and frustration at the bureaucracy and the red tape, you need senior people empowered enough to make decisions to set the stage for success. I work with a range of highly regulated categories, and we can't have a situation where younger, more junior staff are the ones feeling the frustration and banging their heads against a wall. It has to be led from the top-down. You have to have senior stakeholders championing the change and what's required for success. That's the only way change is going to happen. *Joe Petyan, Executive Partner, J Walter Thompson London | @YuriEuro*

The role of the CEO

Too often, the importance of CEOs in digital transformation is underestimated, and their role is relegated to one of the following:

- The permission-giver: where the CEO plays a passive role, required only to give the mandate for digital initiatives, but remains distanced from making it happen and plays little or no involvement beyond initial approval.

- The figurehead: a tactical, skin-deep role, such as giving them a blog or getting them to tweet to provide the *appearance* of supporting your digital agenda, but not really involving them in championing your vision for becoming a digital business or embodying the behaviours that will underpin your culture.

- The endorser: where the CEO's name and the authority of office are used to enable those pushing the digital agenda to overrule colleagues and break through barriers.

In reality, CEOs can be a far more potent change enabler when they are given a more strategic and proactive role in digital transformation and culture – and that role has two key aspects. Firstly, they have an ambassadorial role to play, being seen to embody the behaviours and principles that you are looking to instil organization-wide. Secondly, they must proactively play the role of arbiter among the executive team, ensuring that leaders remain committed to your vision for becoming a digital business and resolving any conflicts or internal barriers.

The CEO as the chief digital ambassador

As we have said, it is not enough to give the CEO a blog or a Twitter account. That may be a digital method, but it is not a digital commitment. It is even worse when such shallow efforts are produced by a marketing, PR or corporate communications team and lack the authenticity of a genuine dialogue from your organization's leader (we have all seen a CEO blog that reads like a press release and has clearly been written by a corporate department, not an individual).

When an organization states an ambition, people instinctively look to its leader for proof, reassurance and a sign of commitment (or lack thereof). Executives, wider employees, customers, investors, analysts and other stakeholders: the potential reach and influence of the CEO or founder is profound, even disproportionate. The term 'leading from the front' is not an empty idea, it is an imperative.

Considering the breadth of an average CEO's responsibilities, he or she cannot be expected personally to oversee all aspects of a digital transformation, but there are several important things the CEO can do to help the organization succeed.

First is **reinforcing the message**. The CEO needs to be a leading storyteller about your digital efforts, repeating and reinforcing your digital vision at every opportunity, both internally and externally. Whether at an all-staff meeting, a company-wide memo, in a blog post or a media interview, reiterating your commitment to digital transformation (and giving examples of progress and accomplishments) will help to build an ongoing storyline that employees see and hear both within the organization, but also from external sources. This repetition will help to drill home how serious the organization is about its stated ambitions and build familiarity with the storyline, enabling others to talk about it in a similar way.

Second is **getting personally involved**. This is not to suggest you should appoint your CEO to sit on a range of project teams, and that is neither practical nor desirable, in many instances. Instead, we are suggesting giving the CEO early-stage access to some key digital developments, or even immersing him or her in a new project before it is shared more widely with a delivery team. The principle of 'showing not telling' will help improve the CEO's understanding of how your investments will make things tangibly better for the company and the customer; provide context (and improved confidence) for when the CEO speaks internally or externally about your digital initiatives; and provide reassurance that their ongoing support is rooted in real outcomes.

Third is **modelling behaviours**. The behaviours, mindsets and ways of working that underpin your vision for becoming a truly digital business need to be embraced throughout the organization, but it is even more critical with your CEO. If your employees do not see evidence of the culture change in the behaviour of their most senior leader, they are likely to view it with scepticism and fail to adopt it themselves. Take your desired behaviours, mindsets and ways of working and look at how you can digitize your CEO's most visible internal and external activities to align with this.

The CEO as the arbiter of your digital vision

One of the things that sets great visions and strategies apart from more mediocre ones is their simplicity. While that is great for telling the story internally and making it meaningful and memorable, it does not reflect the complex realities of implementation.

When CEOs set their leadership team moving in a new direction, the question of 'how to make this happen?' is confronted. And it is at this point that great visions and strategies are most at risk from being watered-down as internal politics, differing opinions and compromises begin to creep in. Here, the CEO needs to be proactive in ensuring that the destination is compromised as it moves from the CEO-mandate to where the rubber meets the road, and this involves three key contributions to making digital transformation a success.

First is **challenging**. The CEO needs to regularly raise the senior team up from the complexities of 'making this happen' to refocus on the big picture, constructively questioning whether, how and how well your digital vision is being translated into action, and provoking healthy discussion and debate and allowing for course-correction over time.

Second is **harmonizing**. Here, the CEO needs to ensure that the senior team is fully aligned with the vision for becoming a digital business. It is not enough for the CEO to say 'this is how it's going to be'… he or she also needs to ensure that the leadership team's personal interpretations, objectives and plans are working in synch.

Third is **resolving**. Disagreements, differing interpretations and ideas, conflicts and tensions are inevitable in any change endeavour. It is the role of the CEO to help tackle these proactively, working to spotlight issues and bring leaders together to tackle them constructively, providing a constant source of independent adjudication and mediation to help reach the best outcome, not the most politically palatable one.

'My challenge is to transform Zurich to be able to compete in the digital world. By the way, I mean the digital world that is here now, not some fantasy in 5 to 10 years' time. And the way that I would articulate you do that, is you start from the top.

'Why? Because, in my opinion, this is a cultural revolution we're trying to achieve, not a technical revolution. That's happening anyway. The challenge is how do we take advantage of it as a business, and make sure we thrive in it, and survive, as opposed to being disrupted.

'And that means a change of mind-set in the culture. In particular, when you're talking about an organization like Zurich, one that's been around for hundreds of years, and has built up lots of heritage, both culturally and technologically and commercially, it's a very difficult thing to do. So for me, the big challenge is aligning the executives of this organization to drive through digital transformation, because me on my own, even with a large team, I'm not going to be able to hit it.

'I need the whole organization aligned, and that is the biggest challenge when you're starting. I would over-emphasize spending more time on doing this, even though that can sound wasteful with the speed of things happening right now, because it will help greatly down the line, when it comes to the implementing and the doing and getting support from across the business.'

Steven Zuanella, Group Chief Digital Officer, RSA Insurance (Steven was Chief Digital Officer at Zurich Insurance plc at the time of this interview)

The reality of trade-offs

As your organization invests in new digital initiatives, it creates the potential for conflict as legacy revenue streams and operations become disrupted or replaced by new digital ones. This can lead to tensions which must be tackled head-on to avoid barriers forming among your leadership team, as some executives push for change while others seek to protect the status quo.

One of the most common trade-offs leaders face is the reallocation of budgets from existing operations to new digital initiatives. This can leave one part of the business that is generating revenues today, having to tighten its belt as budgets are moved to a new digital product or channel. A good example of this is when online shopping was introduced into the grocery retail sector in the early 2000s.

This created several trade-offs for managers to face up to – the first was stock reallocation. Availability is a critical part of the online shopping experience – you want to know that when you order bread and milk for delivery the next morning, you can have certainty that it will be delivered. This means that the retailer's new online channel would have to be given priority over its legacy store operations.

Secondly, online shopping meant that retailers were losing footfall in their stores, and so losing the opportunity for additional sales through impulse purchases, promotional offers and ancillary revenues such as tobacco, lottery, coffee shop and fuel.

Thirdly, online shopping changed many aspects of retailers' operations. New staffing and vehicle requirements emerged as retailers needed to accommodate home delivery drivers. Shift patterns and working practices in distribution needed to change to adapt from delivering solely to retail stores overnight, to delivering to consumers' homes during the day.

Each of these examples created the need for leaders to collectively support changes to the business that had ripple effects elsewhere in the organization. The aim is to get the executive who finds the operations affected by new digital initiatives to a mindset of 'this change is going to have an impact on my part of the business, but it needs to happen and I'm going to support it, even if it makes my life difficult'. And central to doing that, is aligned objectives across the leadership team.

> Figuring out how to survive in a multichannel environment will involve trade-offs, but the last thing you want is to cannibalise existing business. If our move into digital channels, propositions or business models means you're not selling one incremental unit, you're just taking one away from another channel, that's not necessarily a sustainable business model. So the question is, how do you move everyone's attention away from the short-term, me-vs-you mind-set, which only leads to someone winning and someone losing? Instead, how do you focus everyone's attention on working together to find solutions that are going to help the business move forward as a whole, as opposed to trading off channels between each other? *Steven Zuanella, Group Chief Digital Officer, RSA Insurance*

CASE STUDY   Digital technology and banking

Much has been written about the demise of traditional high street banking. First was the arrival of telephone banking in the late 1980s, which began to erode the need for retail branches as many simple transactions such as balance checking or transfers could be done with a phone call, and led to the emergence of a successful new bank launched in the UK in the form of First Direct.

This was followed by internet banking, which while available from the early 1980s in primitive form, found widespread adoption in the early 2000s, further displacing retail branches with desktop access to more sophisticated transaction and account management than provided by telephone banking.

And now, the use of desktop internet banking has fallen for the first time, as the use of mobile banking apps has increased dramatically during the same time period (Milligan, 2016). According to the British Bankers Association (BBA), logins to mobile banking apps increased from 7 million a day in 2014 to 11 million a day in 2015, with customers using such apps a total of 4 billion times over the year.

These technology-driven innovations have had a significantly disruptive effect on banks, fundamentally changing processes, resource requirements, investment and more. In each instance, some executives will have been championing the rationale for change, with others raising concerns about its impact on existing operations.

One area where this shift to new technologies has had a sizeable and direct impact on the banking industry is jobs. In 2013, Barclays announced 1,700 job cuts due to decreasing branch usage and the rise of online banking, and in 2014 Lloyds Banking Group announced a further 9,000 job losses and a range of branch closures due in part to the adoption of new technologies.

Aligning objectives

It is an old cliché: 'what gets measured gets done'. And when it comes to getting your organization committed to your digital vision and the cultural transformation which will support it, objectives are one of the most powerful levers at your disposal.

Digital transformation and culture change cannot be a priority for just one senior manager or function. New digital initiatives require change right across an organization, yet in many instances we find that digital priorities are only reflected in the objectives of the individual appointed to lead the organization's digital agenda (whether that is the Marketing Director, IT Director or a Chief Digital Officer), and by association the function that they represent – and everyone within it.

Consequently, when this individual (let's assume for this example that it is the Chief Digital Officer, or CDO) is pushing to make changes or secure commitment to decisions that may have a negative impact on another function, you may find that leader unwilling to offer support. For instance, let's say the CDO of a bank is pushing to shift budgets from investment in retail branches to a new online channel. The leader in charge of retail branches could be facing a scenario where objectives including product cross-selling through in-branch advertising and branch staff personal selling, are put at risk because the budget needed to achieve them is being diverted elsewhere. Where is the motivation for the leader to support this change? Not only could it affect their division's performance, it could also impact the leader's personal bonus, so it becomes a very real blocker to change, and creates discord among the leadership team.

Having a digital leader, having a digital strategy, and having, from the top, the leadership of the businesses and the core stakeholders all embrace digital. If that isn't the case, then there's going to be stumbling blocks or you'll fall short of what you're trying to achieve. Everyone's got to be aligned within the business. *Charles Yardley, Chief Operating Officer, City AM*

When your organization sets out its digital vision and defines priorities for becoming a truly digital business, it is essential to look at the cross-functional implications, and to ensure that everyone's objectives reflect your stated ambitions – starting with the senior management team, and then cascaded down through each of their functions.

This not only helps to make tensions easier to resolve (or avoid), it also helps an organization to have focus. If your digital vision permeates into the objectives and priorities for each department across the business, managers will be able to look at their plans to ensure that they are contributing to their organization's digital agenda.

The most successful team that I've seen working on digital transformation, is where the CEO and every member of the board around the table agrees, and owns the digital agenda. They don't appoint a CDO and say 'Off you go Steven, you go and sort the digital agenda, we'll support you'. No, no, no. They own the digital agenda as well, showing leadership from the front and treating it as a business imperative, not as a technology, marketing or operations piece that is further down in the organization. *Steven Zuanella, Group Chief Digital Officer, RSA Insurance*

(Non-fiction) Storytelling

One of the keys to getting leadership engagement is helping your senior managers to understand the impact of digital technologies on your organization. Today, few people challenge the ubiquity of digital or its significant impact on the world, but where many people struggle is understanding what these changes mean to them.

We've all seen the 'if Facebook was a country, it would be the biggest in the world' infographics, the mass of great stats at conferences and in presentations about growth rates and adoption rates and so on. What I've seen far less of, in any organization I've been in, is the 'so what'. It's easy to band statistics around but leaders need to hear what this might mean for their customer, their business model and their growth prospects, and there's not enough solid thinking being done on that. *Steven Zuanella, Group Chief Digital Officer, RSA Insurance*

Statistics and evidence is important, but using presentations and swathes of statistics is not the most effective way to get the point across. Research has shown that stories are a more powerful method of conveying information, as they trigger a different response from our brains. This means that a narrative is more important than statistics.

The power of storytelling

How our brains respond to stories

Our brains are far more engaged by storytelling than by cold, hard facts. When reading straight data, only the language parts of our brains work to decode the meaning. But when we read a story, not only do the language parts of our brains light up, but any other part of the brain that we would use if we were actually experiencing what we're reading about becomes activated as well. This means it's far easier for us to remember stories than hard facts. (Gillett, 2014)

Top tips for successful storytelling

If you are trying to influence your top team to support your organization's digital agenda, storytelling and education is critical. Here are some tips to remember when thinking about your approach.

Know your audience. Your senior management team is not one homogeneous group. Team members each have a different level of understanding about digital, and will each have different perspectives and priorities given their position in the organization. This means they will respond to different things, so make sure your storytelling covers a range of different perspectives, or tailor your approach between group sessions and one-to-one discussions.

Anchor everything to the business. Abstract ideas can be difficult for people to relate to, so to avoid misinterpretation, make sure you bring everything back to what this means for your business. For instance, what will a change in customer behaviour mean for how you reach them? What will a change in technology mean for one of your products or services? How will your competitors' digital activities impact your positioning in the market?

Show don't tell. If you are trying to explain something like a new app or a digitized process, don't just talk about it, show people. Rapid prototyping, design concepts, live demos and other visual communication approaches can help simplify the complex and make what you have to say meaningful.

Look inside your own organization. Today, there are five different generations of people in the same workforce, all with very different experiences of digital technologies – some having been born into our connected world (digital natives or GenZ) and some having had to adapt (digital immigrants). How often do you look at your own teams for insight, inspiration and real stories?

Use real people. When trying to educate or engage senior leaders, many people default to statistics, numbers and hard evidence. It is not surprising as it is what we are used to with this audience. Historically, most discussions at the top table have focused on financials, performance, business cases and KPIs, where the requirement for empirical evidence is high. When trying to bring digital to life for leaders, however, more qualitative approaches can be incredibly valuable. Although often dismissed as dated, putting your senior team on the other side of the glass with a focus group can be incredibly powerful, having real customers talking about the role of digital in their lives and their digital experiences with your brand.

Persist and repeat. Some people won't get it first time. Some will need more convincing. Some will buy into your message immediately and others won't even need convincing. Repetition, however, is key. It is not enough to sell an idea to your leaders at the beginning of a journey; you need to keep sharing new insights, new stories and reinforcing the narrative over time.

'It's easy for leadership teams to sit and talk about 'being digital', but I think it's incredibly important for us to first be honest with ourselves about our gaps in knowledge and understanding. Think about the typical composition of a board or executive committee. How many of these people truly live as many of our customers do?

'Understanding our own limitations, as leaders, in terms of our real experience of what our customers are doing every day, is essential. We can then find ways to increase leaders' exposure to customer realities, bring meaningful insights to the top table and connect our leaders with talent in our business who can help close these gaps.

'We recently held some customer discussion groups and the number of our customers that were using special groups they'd set up on WhatsApp, to share, post and commiserate around their bets, winning and losing, was unbelievable. And it was a real eye opener for me. People have talked to

▶

me about it before, but literally, every single person in the two groups we saw that night, of early 20s, had one of these WhatsApp groups.

'I may not live my life on WhatsApp, but some of our customers do. It was a bit of a wake-up call, the realization that we are not bringing that insight into the business at the rate at which we should.'

Kristof Fahy, Chief Marketing Officer, Ladbrokes plc | @kpf1970

'Almost all of the parallels I give to my colleagues are from the private sector. To some extent I talk about some of the things that HMRC, DVLA and others have done to make their services work online, and the way that ours don't yet. But my model of what crime prevention, for example, looks like in the future, is based on Amazon. And we are way off this, but the point about the Amazon model is Amazon use the data that you and I give them through our transactions with them to formulate a profile of us, that enables them proactively to contact us and say, "This time last year, you bought Lee Child's latest book. His new one's just come out. Are you interested?" Or, "It's your friend's birthday. Here's three things your friend would like for their birthday."

'So they're hoovering data, not just from us, but a range of sources, such as social media. My vision of what one aspect of crime prevention looks like in the future, as we develop digital relationships with the public, is in the same way to use that digital data, probably combined with other data, to give people the best possible information to help stop them becoming victims of crime.

'So one level, that could be, "Thomas, you happen to be a BMW driver. We've had a rash of BMWs stolen in your area of London. They're getting in by doing X, Y, and Z. The way to deal with this is to A, B and C. Some of the data that would help us to help you avoid having your BMW stolen we already have, because we have the crime data already. What we don't have is the digital relationship with people that would enable us to identify the group who are most likely to be vulnerable to having their car stolen.

'And if I'm trying to communicate that to our leaders or colleagues, I say "imagine applying Amazon, that methodology, to the way we engage to the public".'

Martin Fewell, Director of Media and Communications, The Metropolitan Police | @martinfewell

Key points

- A united and aligned leadership team is essential to build a digital culture and for the ongoing success of any digital transformation initiatives.

- The role of the CEO in your digital agenda risks being relegated to that of a figurehead, permission-giver or passive-endorser, whereas CEOs are far more effective in making change happen when involved more proactively as both 'chief digital ambassador' and as arbiter of your digital vision.

- New digital initiatives have ripple effects throughout a business, often leading to the need to make trade-offs on budgets, resourcing, prioritization, staffing and other areas, creating the potential for conflict and tensions among leaders as some executives push for change while others seek to protect the status quo.

- Aligning objectives at the top table is essential for securing a shared commitment to your digital agenda – it cannot sit just with one executive. Your digital ambitions need to be reflected in the goals and KPIs of your entire senior management team, and then cascaded down through all of their functions.

- Storytelling is essential for engaging leaders in your digital aspirations and helping to educate as to what the changing world of digital technology means for your business and its future prospects.

Agility 11

One of the characteristics that most distinguishes smaller, digitally oriented start-ups from larger, established and legacy businesses, is pace and agility.

Smaller organizations do not have years of legacy to contend with. They are free to act quickly and decisively, can pivot at a moment's notice, are more receptive to experimentation and do not fear failure.

Larger or more established businesses, on the other hand, typically spend years defining processes, governance, bureaucracy and policies, often for good reason. Process, governance and the like enable accountability. They bring transparency. They help mitigate risk. They provide oversight and control. These are not bad things in principle, but in practice, they can quickly become major barriers for organizations that are trying to undertake a digital transformation.

The answer, inevitably, is about balance. You do not want to throw the baby out with the bathwater and eliminate or override all of your internal controls and processes indiscriminately. Equally, you do not want to force your digital initiatives to conform to a system that will hold back potential and hamper success.

> Speed is essential. The world is moving very quickly and experiencing a profound level of disruption. Organizations of all sizes need to be able to pivot quickly as new technologies and new coding languages change the way we approach digital. *Russ Shaw, Founder, Tech London Advocates | @RussShaw1*

The need for speed

One of the main promises of digital technology is its rapid, real-time nature. Performance data are at your fingertips 24 hours a day. Prototyping and developing new websites, apps and digital communications tools can be done in days and weeks, not the months associated with traditional product development. Market testing and feedback can be immediate, not subject to the lags associated with product launches and subsequent focus group feedback.

One of the challenges businesses face, however, is that they are often not geared up to be as responsive as digital allows you to be. You can see real-time how people are interacting with your website, for instance, and spot potential issues or areas that could be optimized, but how do you address it? It might be flagged for review by a relevant colleague who owns that proposition, before a change request or ticket is logged with a different department that will queue it, after which it will be actioned according to an internal service level agreement. It might then make its way back to someone in marketing for approval before going live, and that might not be instant either – it could be 48 hours later at the next live environment release.

That may read like something of an extreme example but in reality, for many people it will read true. Meanwhile, days could have gone by and either the issue has continued to persist, or the opportunity has been missed. For established businesses, that process was created for a reason. To stop unfettered access to your digital shop window and avoid change conflicts. To ensure appropriate stakeholder sign-offs with an audit trail to back it up.

But in the digital world we are in, this snail-pace simply will not work. What is the point in having access to live, real-time digital performance analytics if you cannot take advantage of it?

'If you're running a digital business, it's very much an iterative approach to improvement. It's constant fine tuning, it's constant changing, whether it be marketing, customer experience, conversion or merchandising. The learning experience never ends.

'In a number of industries that are new to digital, data is not available in real time, sometimes there can be a six week lag. In traditional bricks retailing, you tend to operate on a weekly cycle around Monday morning meetings discussing trading that happened from the Monday through to the Sunday. So that's a week out. In the online grocery business that we ran at Morrison's, we were doing sales three times a day, and at lastminute.com we did it every hour. Massive, massive, massive differences in terms of behaviour, management reporting and – critically – speed of decision making.'

Simon Thompson, Global Head of Digital Commerce, HSBC PLC

If we don't continually respond to the signals that digital gives us, someone else will. Large, established organizations, once thought the leaders of their industry, are under attack from nimble, pacey start-ups that seem to come from nowhere but can outmanoeuvre legacy businesses to impressive effect.

Just ask Michael Dubin and Mark Levine, the founders of Dollar Shave Club. Five years after the entrepreneurs shook up the shaving market with a radically different, digitally powered business model, Unilever has announced it intends to purchase them for a whopping billion-dollar price tag. Unilever, it should be noted, competes directly with one of the victims of Dollar Shave Club's disruption, Procter & Gamble, the owner of shaving brand Gillette.

Further supporting the importance of speed to cope with digitally driven change, results from a recent McKinsey Global Survey that 43 per cent of high performers from their research say their companies take digital initiatives from idea to implementation in less than six months, while only 17 per cent of all other respondents report the same (Bughin *et al*, 2015).

Think like a start-up

Pace and agility are intuitive to digitally oriented start-ups. They live and breathe agile development, jams, hacks and other rapid response ideals because they do not know any different.

Ask yourself, how would we approach this project if we were independent of our wider organization? If we had all of the resource we needed but none of the constraints that hold us back? What would be different about your approach?

What would this newfound freedom enable us to do quicker or better, but where might we be vulnerable? How can you find the best of both worlds?

> If you draw a graph of the acceleration of business and consumer change and demand, it's growing almost exponentially. And we're not catching up. So what's happening is that gap's getting bigger by the day, in terms of metabolic rate and in terms of agility. And what you see with these garages, startups and entrepreneurs, is that they have the agility. They make decisions on the spot. They don't have massive bureaucracies to go through. They don't have steering group after steering group. They have agile, scrum, fail fast, entrepreneurial spirit, and risk management. *Steven Zuanella, Group Chief Digital Officer, RSA Insurance*

Overcoming the barriers

Pace is not just about mindset, though, it is also about process. It is one thing to mandate your teams to be more responsive and nimble, but if you do not remove the blockages and barriers in the system which slows them down, you will be left with an empty aspiration and some rather frustrated colleagues.

Think about how decisions get made. In many organizations, projects must adhere to a governance system which includes committees and sign-off groups. These committees typically meet on a monthly or quarterly basis, so if you are tasking a team to work in an agile, pacey way on a new app development, for example, the team will be keen to get something proto-typed and ready for testing in-market. Do you then stall progress for weeks until the next formal committee meeting, or do you need to find a better way to make governance work for you, not the other way round?

> If I had a pound for every time there has been a great idea that a team, both client and agency side, believe would be great to do, and then you're either beaten to market by somebody else or it just simply doesn't get off the ground because of the treacle, and the systems, and the lack of enablement in a company. It happens so, so often. So the appetite is there, the will is there, the ideas are all there, but without the systems and the infrastructure to allow it to happen, then it's all for naught. *Joe Petyan, Executive Partner, J Walter Thompson London | @YuriEuro*

To tackle this, start small and start early. Take live priorities and planned projects and ask yourself what steps you need to go through internally to get things done.

- Who needs to be involved to help get a project ready for launch decision?
- What sign-off processes do you have to work to?
- What departments have to countersign a project before it is ready to go live?
- Is there anyone you should consult with to smooth the path ahead for the project?
- Which are the most time-consuming parts of our internal process and what impact do they have on our project?
- Where are we most likely to find delays or internal barriers?

By identifying key internal stakeholders and processes early on, you are able to get ahead of potential surprises further down the line which could delay or derail your project, and you can find ways to work around these barriers. Bringing stakeholders into your project at the beginning helps to build shared understanding of what you are trying to do and why, and helps you to build shared ownership of making it a success.

'Once you get everyone to a point where they realize that we need to think about how we can increase the cadence of change within the organization, then it's a case of breaking down the organizational silos and trying to break down some of the governance structures that we've got in place. In the very early days of identifying the new digital ideas and concepts we want to pursue, we make sure that we've got cross-functional representation as we develop those ideas.

'We want everyone to buy in from day one, and make sure everyone has got skin in the game from the outset. We identify any hurdles, showstoppers or blockers that might be thrown at us by the regulator or by our risk teams, security teams, fraud teams, compliance teams or legal teams, whatever it might be. We flush those out nice and early, but everyone has ownership of that. Everyone sees what the big goal is, and we just work collaboratively throughout the cycle to make sure that we can move at pace, address hurdles as quickly as possible, get that idea to a concept or a prototype and then start testing with customers as quickly as possible.'

Ian Morgan, Managing Director, Digital Channels, Barclays UK

Decision rights

One way to improve pace and agility, is to rethink your decision rights. Put simply, that means looking at who has the authority to make what sort of decisions, and when. Too often, especially with projects that have a high level of investment or perceived risk, decision rights are retained by people in senior-level positions, which can create delays and time-lags, and this usually occurs for one of three reasons.

First, *legacy*. If decisions at every stage of a project are rolled-up to upper management to approve or validate, it will continue to apply to your digital initiatives and projects. Why wouldn't it? It has always been that way.

Second, *self-preservation*. Particularly when dealing with the unknowns that often accompany digital investments, more junior project team members might want to indemnify themselves from any failures or underperformance. 'I'm not shouldering this burden alone.'

Third, *self-interest*. Senior executives may delegate digital projects to lower levels in an organization, but they will often retain a personal interest and overenthusiasm in how it is progressing, the choices being made along the way and the landmark decisions that might become historically significant for their organization. Ultimately, they want to be hands-on when it comes to the important decisions, but hands-off with the legwork.

Empowering a team to progress key digital initiatives and to do so with agility, pace and responsiveness means they need to be trusted. Trusted to be diligent in their analysis and robust in their process of evaluation.

We are not saying that digital leaders and teams should be given full autonomy to make all of the calls as they see fit with no oversight or governance. Instead, we are recommending a pragmatic review of which choices are best made by individuals or teams working on a project to give them the pace, flexibility and decisiveness that they need, while only the most critical decision points are brought to a wider group of stakeholders. Ultimately, it is about finding a better balance between the two.

Failing fast

Failure has too much stigma attached to it, and a cultural volte-face is needed.

If you are trying to create a pacier, more agile business culture to support your digital transformation, you need to get your people comfortable with the idea of making mistakes, and your leaders comfortable with the idea that your legacy approach to developing new product or services needs to change. This is not to say that failure should be celebrated, rather that in today's fast-moving and uncertain digital world, mistakes are inevitable – we just need to ensure we learn from them, and quickly.

The investments you will make in new digital technologies and ways of working bring with them uncertainty. There are more unknowns today than ever before, as technology and the competitive and customer context in which you operate continues to evolve. At the heart of 'failing fast' is recognizing that it is better to get a concept or prototype to 80 per cent perfection, get it out to customers and learn from a live environment, than to delay for weeks and months trying to build in guarantees and certainties that are largely unachievable. This runs counter to how most organizations have historically operated, using lengthy and often complex product and project review cycles to eke out as much risk as possible. It is better today to build something you know to be imperfect, but let (in a controlled way) your customers or users guide you on what to improve and why. They will typically identify more and possibly different issues quicker than you could capture in internal reviews that take markedly longer.

We're in this strange world where historically it all was about proof, having evidence and data in order to let you make the next step in your business or in your marketing. Now we're in a world where you have to take the plunge first and see what happens. It's more experimental, it's more test and learn. It's more about a leap of faith. And I think it's the people who take the risks, and believe, and take a leap of faith that are the ones who succeed. If you sit back, wait, want to validate, want to test, want to stress test, someone else will have innovated faster, and got to market quicker, and done something better by the time you get to it. I really do believe this leap of faith notion is so, so important in the digital world. The speed, the responsiveness and the dynamism of everything allows you to dip your toe in the water and get going, rather than testing to death and finding yourself three years out of date before you've even begun. *Joe Petyan, Executive Partner, J Walter Thompson London | @YuriEuro*

To support this approach, first *ensure that you are not punishing failure.* Make sure that people and departmental objectives, targets and KPIs do not run counter to a mandate to embrace failure and risk individuals fearing a test-and-learn ethos for failure of consequence.

Second, *make sure you codify learnings.* Making mistakes is fine, it is repeating them which is problematic. Establish a mechanism by which bugs and glitches are documented into a body of knowledge that can be revisited and taken into account in future projects.

Third, *make sure you are set up to react.* If you know you will need to iterate your project, make sure you have got resource from the right people and times lined up to assess learnings and address them swiftly, and keep both your colleagues and customers updated with how you are responding to feedback.

With the web, you can afford to continuously test and innovate and try different approaches. The web is a self-correcting mechanism. It's different to the print world where if you write something that's inaccurate, you can't go back and take it out, but you can very quickly change that online. *Charles Yardley, Chief Operating Officer, City AM*

Agile methodology, reapplied

Agility may be a concept, but agile is also a methodology. If you have come across it before, it is likely you found it in your IT department.

Agile is an alternative approach to traditional project management. It is used as a more fluid, iterative approach than traditional 'waterfall' development, where the process is more linear and sequential. It is well suited to uncertain and unpredictable environments, which is why it is ideal for digital transformation.

The very term 'transformation', and talk of visions and strategies, can feel overwhelming. It implies something substantial, something significant, and something complex. And while that may be the reality of the change facing your organization, it does not all have to come at once. In fact, breaking the substantial, the significant and the complex down into manageable, bitesize chunks is essential if you want to get off the whiteboard and into action.

Agile helps you to prioritize the right projects rather than under-resource too many. It helps you to put the right people on the right projects, and give them the bandwidth to deliver. It helps to avoid overbearing governance, instead using the principles of empowerment and lean working to prioritize working sessions rather than countless meetings. It keeps leaders at the right distance from operational decision-making, focusing their involvement on adding value rather than trying to manage and get involved. It ensures that decisions are respected as decisions, preventing marginal ideas from resurfacing after being reviewed and discounted. It reduces cumbersome review cycles and oversight to help foster pace.

Leader's perspective: Gordon Nardini, Travelport

'I truly believe there's a death of the 12-month planning process. Nothing changes from 31 December to 1 January, it's a continuation of your customer's journey, therefore you need to be agile in what you do. That means you've got to continually be testing and understanding your customer journey, continually testing that you're meeting customer needs.

'So in our organization we now use Kanban boards, which came from work on manufacturing processes in Japan, we use continual sprints in our marketing organization, and we will phase out the legacy 12-month plan and quarterly reviews as the wider business embraces these techniques.

'We have monthly sprints which set out what we're going to deliver and what we're going to do, and we can pivot on a sixpence if there's a change in the global macroeconomic environment, if we need to respond to a competitor action, or if the initial validation with customers doesn't meet our expectations. And this is incredibly powerful for digital, where we need to get things out to market quickly, to learn from them and to be able to respond at a pace that traditional planning didn't typically suit.

'So we've employed lean manufacturing principles which underpin agile methodology, into what we call "lean marketing". We use those four-week sprints to deliver things in-market with focus... short, sharp and to the point, but we also have a continual backlog which is what you might have historically called a marketing plan. This means we always have a six-month context, but when it comes to implementation, we're focused on those shorter, sharper interventions and we're not tied to any investments or activities which would be difficult to unpick if conditions or priorities take a sudden change.

'I truly believe that for marketing teams to embrace disruption and help deliver a digital transformation for their business, they need to embrace agile methodologies and principles. This is a major change, but one which will enable you to pivot quickly and respond to the changing competitive, economic and market conditions you're faced with. And in the face of such constant change, this way of working can be incredibly valuable.

'We borrowed this way of working from Travelport's Labs division that use agile for product innovation. They kill more ideas than they progress but they use this methodology for ideation, rapid concept development, testing and market fit and we now do the same in marketing. If we launch a campaign and it's a disaster, we can kill it. We don't cross our fingers for three or six months and keep telling ourselves it's "just a slow uptake"; we develop ideas, we get them out in market and we see what happens, but we're always poised to pivot and respond and it's a fundamentally different way of working.

'This way of working enables us to spend significantly less, developing a campaign concept, getting it in market and responding accordingly. If it works, we accelerate it, we invest in it and we scale it. If not, we move on to the next thing, having not lost significant time and significant money.

'If you truly want to make digital transformation a success, agile methodology will help you to improve pace and agility without compromising strategic direction, and I believe that it's a key way of working to create the culture that a truly digital business needs.'

Gordon Nardini, Senior Director, Marketing, Travelport plc | @flufforfact

Key points

- Digital technology provides instant, real-time insights into customer behaviour and market performance, but many organizations are not geared up to be as responsive as this might enable them to be. Organizations need to respond to the signals that digital offers and think like a start-up to find ways to become more fleet-of-foot.

- Identify key stakeholders and internal processes and controls early on in a project and bring together cross-functional teams to create shared ownership of success, and to identify blockers and barriers before they derail or delay initiatives.

- Review who has the authority to make which decisions, and when. Find a better balance in your decision rights to allow projects to operate with pace, flexibility and responsiveness, while applying oversight and escalation to wider stakeholders for the most critical decisions.

- Failure has too much of a stigma in businesses and this needs a cultural volte-face. Failing fast is a key ingredient of a digital culture – not celebrating mistakes but making them quickly, learning from them, and moving on. Ensure your departmental and team objectives and KPIs do not punish those who embrace this, codify learnings from the good and the bad, and make sure your teams are resourced to react to what they learn and iterate digital projects promptly.

- Adopt the principles of agile methodology to infuse speed and nimbleness into your digital transformation efforts. Use it to overcome cumbersome planning and to balance the need for oversight and governance with agility and rapid concept development, prototyping and customer testing.

Environment 12

If you want to build a digital culture and attract great digital talent, you need foosball tables, a restored 1980s Pac Man arcade game, and a tolerance for shorts and flip-flops in the workplace. Agree or disagree?

While this may seem a bit flippant, the environment that your people work in can have a material impact on your employees' behaviours, either reinforcing or undermining your stated ambitions, and therefore influencing the culture you are trying to engender. For instance, let's say you want to promote collaborative ways of working, but your office environment consists of seas of cubicles or closed offices, with no shared working areas or open meeting spaces. One conflicts the other, no?

While Google and Facebook have popularized 'funky' working environments for the digital generation in recent years, the allure of a contemporary, relaxed working environment has gone beyond being in vogue or a bit of a gimmick, to become something of a proxy for the culture and style of an organization.

As businesses look to attract the same digital talent that is also being courted by start-ups, entrepreneurs and tech giants, not to mention the growing appeal of independent working from a young age, they are having to adapt to new generations that shun suits and career tracks for portfolio projects and a sense of career freedom.

And it is not just recruitment of digitally oriented talent where this comes to the fore. Legacy businesses that are encouraging their employees to adapt to new working styles in support of building a truly digital business are finding that they need to back up their new mantras with tangible evidence of the type of organization they want to become, and the work environment is one very effective way of doing just that.

Culture and environment

As in nature itself, people respond to the environment they are placed in. The conditions in which we spend most of our waking hours and operate in has a fundamental influence on how we act and behave. Let's look at some of the common characteristics of a successful digital culture and how our working environments either support or conflict with them.

First is *collaboration*. As part of your digital agenda, you need your people to work more effectively across functional and divisional boundaries and silos. To support this in the working environment, you might employ open plan offices to remove barriers to communication; opportunities for hot desking, to encourage people to work alongside a variety of different colleagues, rather than have their immediate sphere of contact limited to the same handful of people; open plan and shared meeting spaces, to encourage people to interact with different teams and spot opportunities to share and connect on different projects; and dedicated spaces or meeting zones with planning boards, ideation rooms and workshop toolkits.

Second is *pace*. You want to encourage more pace in project teams and decision-making, so you might look to your working environment to help eliminate delays brought on by review meetings and committees. Instead of scheduling meetings and developing presentations, you might create live project zones within your work environment, using storyboards, war rooms and project walls to chart project work in a live and visible way. When you need to get someone's input on an issue, provide a project update or seek feedback or approval on something, you bring colleagues to the project zone for a discussion, potentially significantly reducing the time it would otherwise take to have the same conversation in a more formal setting. Equally, you might improve pace by introducing a more flexible use of your workspace, where you are able to easily move people around to form different project teams in close proximity, and then reshuffle as needed, without the usual strain that comes with less flexible office moves.

Third is *transparency*. You want to promote more visibility of your digital agenda and how key initiatives are progressing, so you might look to your work environment as an internal communication channel. Simple yet effective approaches here include making the best use of your wall space to share information and reinforce messaging. Internally advertising your digital vision and key priorities on office walls, effective signposting to give project teams identities and placing digital KPI dashboard posters in internal meeting spaces and online in intranets and digital workspaces are all common approaches.

Before you start removing cubicle walls or having your digital mission painted on the office wall, it is worth grounding what sceptics might see as frivolous or gimmicky activities in some clear aims, using the following questions:

- What are the ways of working we are trying to instil to promote an effective digital culture?
- How do our people interact today – what are the working norms in our business?
- Which of these are supportive of the actions and behaviours we are trying to encourage? How can we do more of them?
- Which of these conflict with the actions and behaviours we are trying to encourage? How can we change them?
- What opportunities do we have within our working environment and practices to help ignite our digital transformation?

We leveraged a couple of projects to help initiate our digital transformation, and set the tone for the digital culture we wanted to create. The first involved developing our intranet – what we see as part of our digital working environment – from a very basic system to one that has the social collaboration tools that allow people to network within an organization. It sounds obvious, but up until we did this, we didn't allow people from our own organization to post onto the internet, except in very limited circumstances and usually moderated by us. Historically we'd seen social functionality and social media as a risk to the organization both internally and externally, but in recognizing that we're in a more open, connected world and bringing that into the organization and how our people collaborate and communicate, we were able to show our commitment to change. *Martin Fewell, Director of Media and Communications, The Metropolitan Police | @martinfewell*

Digital technology and the workplace

When you visit Twitter's London office, you sign in at reception on an iPad. When you visit Google's London office, you check in at a digital screen and your host is automatically notified. You wouldn't expect anything less, would you? They're digital companies, aren't they? In fact, if you had to sign a comparatively old-school visit logbook (in triplicate), you might smile to yourself and find it a tad ironic.

Signing in to reception may seem a small, if not trivial, example, but when we think about reinforcing a digital culture through the work environment, it is important to think about the employee (and indeed visitor) experience.

If you are setting out an agenda to transform into a truly digital business, over time the fruits of your initial projects and initiatives will start to gain momentum. The vision for becoming digital will start to become a reality, which will start to highlight aspects of your business that still feel 'a bit analogue'. By looking at the design and features of your work environment, you will be able to identify opportunities to digitize which can be both efficient (saving time or money) and symbolic (proof points that your digital ambition is real).

Whether it's digital reception sign-ins, screens in meeting rooms to make presentations and co-working easier, or digital wallets for your staff cafeteria, consider the following questions to help identify opportunities to digitize your work environment:

- What are the typical day-to-day employee and visitor experiences of our workplace like?
- Where are the key touchpoints where we could make a difference with digital technology?
- Which of these opportunities can reduce time or money, and which can be symbolic of our digital agenda? Ideally, where can we find opportunities that combine both?

Competing for digital talent

One of the realities facing businesses seeking digital talent today lies in generational differences. Generation Z, or the 'iGeneration', a group generally seen as born in the late 1990s and early 2000s, is the first generation to be considered truly digitally native.

This generation shares many of the characteristics of the preceding generation, millennials, in that attitudes to education, employment and purpose in life are markedly different from Gen X and Baby Boomers. These people are jaded, cynical, entrepreneurial, nomadic, technologically dependent and civically conscious. But they have also a far stronger grasp of digital technology, as it has been omnipresent for most, if not all, of their lives.

Add to that the new 'cool' jobs in coding and digital product management, and the growing appeal of independent working and starting a business, and you have some interesting talent issues to consider.

First, this group is *hard to attract*. Large, established or legacy businesses might struggle to appeal to the digital talent of this generation, when compared with the start-up and entrepreneurial alternatives. You have to contend with the allure of flexible working in 'cool' start-up environments like Shoreditch and Silicon Roundabout in London or Silicon Valley in

California. You have to convince someone to join an organization and work on projects for the business, rather than building and monetizing apps for themselves. You have to contend with the bidding war that can ensue for top digital talent, with some specialists commanding six-figure salaries at an early age, because demand is high and (in the UK in particular) supply is weak.

Second, this group is *hard to retain*. The iGeneration leans more towards project and portfolio based roles than careers. There is greater comfort with a lack of job security and more of a passion for doing projects that add value to a portfolio than in developing a career track with one business. What is more, the specialized nature of a number of digital and digital marketing roles inherently limits career progression as there is little scope for promotion in such a niche field. From our interviews with digital leaders for this book, we were told of numerous examples of people joining an organization to work on a project for six or nine months, and then leaving for no other reason than they wanted to work on a different type of project. Not a case of not liking the organization or the team, or for lack of opportunity – just that they felt like moving on to another interesting project elsewhere.

This means that attracting digital talent from the iGeneration requires a different concept of a 'package' and benefits, and the work environment is one area that established businesses may need to revisit.

Beware the cool kids in the corner

When building a digital team and capability, it is important to avoid a clash of cultures. As businesses increasingly hire new digital talent in software engineering, iOS app development, product management and other fields, you often see a change in working environment and practices. As we have discussed, when you are recruiting from a very different generation and competing with start-up and Silicon Valley-esque cultures, many businesses are having to relax their more formal or corporate ways of working to attract and motivate these individuals.

While there will always be intergenerational and functional differences in an organization, it is especially important when undertaking a digital transformation and culture change endeavour not to create (the feeling of) a two-tiered system. Any nuances in the working environment and working practices that are put in place to cultivate the right talent in your digital teams, need to be offset by a coherent story to the wider organization about the value this group brings to the future success of the business, and efforts to ensure that these employees are integrated into the organization, and not managed as a semi-independent entity.

'One of the things that was said to me in my recruitment phase was, "if digital becomes the cool kids in the corner, we fail". We've worked hard to avoid this happening and, while some of our new working practices and cultural change efforts created some friction in the early days, it's really settled down now.

'One real life example of how even small cultural changes caused friction would be in the impact of our change of dress code. One of the first things we did as part of our transformation journey was to get rid of the rigid, formal dress code across the business. We knew that the kind of people we needed to hire to drive our digital transformation would be put off by an environment with overly corporate or stuffy rules. Whilst this move applied to everyone across the business, it did lead to some cultural whiplash with existing employees. Across the office, we went from everyone in suits to having a whole bunch of new guys coming in in shorts and flip flops almost overnight. Looking back, it's unsurprising that such a sudden change to accepted practices drew a lot of questions and, at times, consternation.

'It took time to resolve some of the cultural friction challenges, but we've worked hard to eliminate sources of tension. Key to this was a big focus on engaging with key stakeholders and building relationships. The more time we spent setting out our agenda and explaining why we worked the way we did, the more aligned we became across the business. In addition to this, the organization has now really embraced a new strategy that has digital and customer at the heart and so we are all now focused behind a common vision. It's had quite a galvanizing effect on how we work together.'

Dominic Grounsell, Global Marketing Director, Travelex | @DomGrounsell

Key points

- Identify how your work environment either supports or conflicts with the digital culture you are trying to create. Identify how changes to working practices and workplace norms can improve collaboration, pace and transparency.

- Review the typical day-to-day employee and visitor experiences of your workplace. Look for key touchpoints where you could make a difference with digital technology, either reducing time or money and/or being symbolic of your digital agenda.

- Digital talent, particularly from the iGeneration, is both hard to attract and hard to retain. Rethink the concept of a job package and benefits and explore how the working environment you create for these roles and teams aligns with their values and characteristics as a generation.

- Avoid digital teams becoming isolated from the organization or seen as the 'cool kids in the corner'. Create the right environment for them to thrive but ensure their value is clearly articulated to the business, and that they are integrated rather than left too independent.

Skills and talent 13

With an environment of constant change and a need for internal agility, the people in our teams and their skills and abilities will determine our success. The greatest strategy in the world is no good without the resources to deliver it, but it is no longer as simple as putting together a job spec and just recruiting people with the right skills and experience. The skills needed today will morph and change in the coming months and years, until our skillsets from five years ago will seem archaic very quickly.

This need for constantly evolving skills poses a number of challenges. Developing the right criteria and processes for recruitment is something we will address in this chapter, but this is actually one of the easier parts of the process (although critically important). The more challenging areas are how do we encourage existing staff to develop their skills and how do we take people on a journey of change with their skills, when they may be utterly resistant to the change in the first place?

Resistance to change

Resistance to change is nothing new or surprising. As human beings, we are generally inclined, by our genetics, to minimize doing anything risky. If we have a role or particular tasks that we have been doing successfully for some time, changing how we do it could lead to different outcomes and different outcomes are potentially risky. We therefore get into habits of doing things a certain way, and we develop a comfort zone around doing things in this way. Generally, learning something new involves expanding out of our comfort zone and that takes committed effort, again something that we tend to shy away from, as committed effort uses up precious resources such as time and concentration. It is therefore not surprising that many of us will find reasons and excuses not to learn new things. We could all speak many languages if we decided to commit the appropriate time and resources into learning them. However, most of us do not speak a dozen different languages, because, relatively speaking, it would be hard work. So, how do we create a culture that encourages this learning behaviour at every stage of our careers?

Complete resistance

What do you do when you come across someone, or even worse, a team of people, who refuse to come along on the digital transformation journey? The key is understanding the cause of their resistance, and normally this comes from one of a very limited number of places. Generally, people feel threatened by the change. They feel threatened that their role or skills are no longer needed. The key to making things work and bring them on the journey successfully is communication. Take a look at Chapter 15, Translation and communication, in this Part.

There will, however, be some people who refuse to change. This may be because they fundamentally think it is a bad idea or that they are near retirement and see little reason to change. Again, the first stage is communication and full understanding of their viewpoint. However, we should always remember that if the organization is to survive it needs to change, and the harsh reality is that people who stall that process threaten the entire organization. Leadership is key to communicating the importance and need for any changes, so make sure you review chapters 9–13, Essentials, in this Part.

Learning techniques

One of the key challenges of learning new skills is the techniques themselves we use in order to acquire the skill in the first place. Many of us go on training courses, feel that we have learned lots of useful new things, only to return to work to carry on in exactly the same patterns of behaviour, and within a few weeks, our new learnings are forgotten. The problem here is the learning technique. It is not that training courses are intrinsically bad, it is just that they are separate from our day-to-day roles. We very often leave our place of work, leave our day-to-day activities, and do something different for a day. Training courses are often seen as a benefit, a day out and sometimes, a bit of an easy day. Training should be fun, as it means you are more likely to learn that way, but they also need to be built into our day-to-day roles. We need training to be embedded into our normal activities. We need a commitment that every time we learn something new, we look at how it could benefit our organization, we plan and implement an experiment to see how it may be implemented and then we look at the results to see how we might further expand the experiment.

Experiments in the workplace

To develop an effective approach to training and skills, we need an organizational commitment to trying out ideas. If I go on a training course and then come back and suggest we change our entire process for selling, it is unlikely I will get buy-in to make that change immediately. It is just too big an undertaking to be made on the opinion of one person, based on something we learned on a course (or read in an article, etc). However, if I come back from a training course and I suggest a test to investigate how successful a new sales process might be, I am much more likely to get buy-in. These tests are basically experiments, and the definition of an experiment is something we should embrace. An experiment is defined as 'a scientific procedure undertaken to make a discovery, test a hypothesis, or demonstrate a known fact'. To define it a bit further, scientific is defined as 'systematic; methodical'. So we need to plan methodical procedures to test our hypothesis that a new sales process will improve our sales.

This culture of experimentation has to be in place to encourage this response to new information. What can we do to test whether this will work in a reasonably risk-free way? This is a question we should be asking constantly and we should be encouraging others to be asking as well. But as well as asking the question and planning our experiments, we need the environment and resources in which these can be carried out. We need to define the sign-off process, have a defined risk-assessment process and have assigned resources for carrying out these kinds of projects. We need to define how much of our time should be spent on experiments versus what we normally do on a day-to-day basis. All of this takes planning, process and iteration, so make sure that you read Chapter 17, Process and governance, as well.

Learning techniques also cannot be limited to training courses. Things change constantly and we cannot constantly be out of the office on training courses; we need a range of learning techniques to help us assimilate the latest techniques and skills as part of our day-to-day role. We will explore all of these different techniques later in this chapter.

T-shaped people

Beyond the learning techniques and commitment to experimentation and implementation, we need to focus on the types of people we are recruiting and developing. The concept of a T-shaped person is not about their physical appearance, but rather the profile of their skills. The idea is that we need staff with a deep knowledge of their given area of expertise (this is represented by the straight vertical line of the T) as well as broad knowledge that they can apply to solve a wide range of problems (this is represented by the horizontal line of the T). The need for these broad skills is based on the reality that as the environment we work in changes, we need to solve new problems we have not encountered before, and by using a broad skillset these problems do become road blocks to our progress.

To assist everyone to be more T-shaped, we can provide a culture of innovation that encourages experimentation with new solutions, as well as providing learning resources so that people can continuously improve their skills. Review the training solutions below to see which techniques are well suited to helping provide new skills on an ongoing basis.

The digital skills gap

Around 40 per cent of digital entrepreneurs say that they face challenges finding skilled digital workers (Tech City, 2016). The discipline of digital marketing in particular is changing constantly and the pace of change continues to increase. 'Digital marketing' also covers a wide range of disciplines, including very broad topics like Social Media, which means that the need for these skills is impacting on a wide range of roles well beyond marketers. Managers of all types need to understand the impact that new technologies may have on their organizations, and pretty much every member of staff will need to understand the fundamentals of the web and social media. As such, increasing numbers of people are looking to improve their skills and trying to keep them up to date. In this section we will explore the best ways of improving our own skills or how we can help our teams to improve their skills. We will then look at the best ways of keeping these skills up to date and relevant.

Digital marketing training and jobs

It is interesting to note that the level of searches for digital marketing jobs (Figure 13.1) is far higher than, but pretty much in line with, the searches for digital training and courses. You can also see in the word cloud in

Figure 13.1 Searches for digital marketing jobs (top line), digital marketing courses (middle line) and digital marketing training (bottom line) in Google from Google Trends

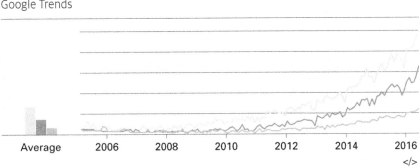

| Average | 2006 | 2008 | 2010 | 2012 | 2014 | 2016 |

</>

Figure 13.2 (from the excellent *Brandwatch social media analysis tool*), when we analysed a huge range of terms related to the topic, the most popular terms related to training and job roles (and interestingly work/life balance, which we will return to later).

Figure 13.2 Word cloud showing most often mentioned phrases over a one-month period related to digital skills

SOURCE: Brandwatch

Figure 13.3 Global mentions over 61 days of terms related to digital skills on social media

| World Overview (Mentions Map) | Improving digital skills | Last 61 days |

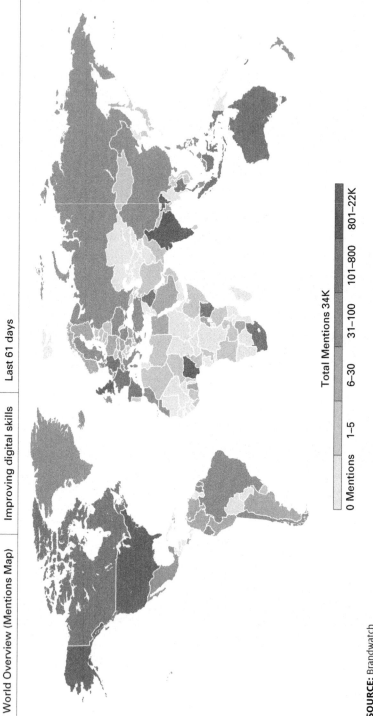

Total Mentions 34K

| 0 Mentions | 1–5 | 6–30 | 31–100 | 101–800 | 801–22K |

SOURCE: Brandwatch

Global digital marketing skills shortage

The global chart (Figure 13.3) does not show any great surprises, with English-speaking countries including the United Kingdom, United States, Canada and Australia having the highest level of conversations, but many European countries are also discussing digital skills in English. This reflects our practical experience that many people are struggling to find training in their own region and are travelling to the United Kingdom for training. We can also see the huge demand for improving knowledge in India.

Figure 13.4 Most active days of the week to engage around digital skills-related topics

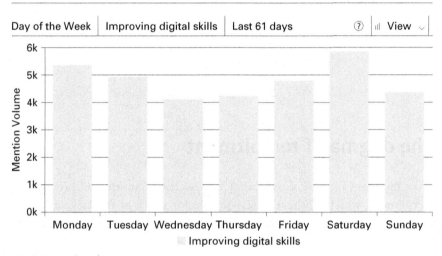

SOURCE: Brandwatch

The insights of day of week (Figure 13.4) and time of day (Figure 13.5) are in line with our previous research and practical experience. That is, that people are using their morning commute time to try to improve their skills via blogs, podcast, tweets, etc, and that upon reaching work, particularly on a Monday morning, one of the first things that many of us do is to search for a new job! This actually makes perfect sense, as once you are sick of your job, Monday mornings are generally the toughest part of the week! What actionable insights can we take from this? First of all, if you are sending a recruitment message, do it on a Monday morning. Secondly, educational content around job skills works first thing in the morning, so we can absorb it when we travel. You can also see a peak at weekends, when people may take some time out to try to improve their skills.

Figure 13.5 Most active time of day to engage around digital skills-related topics

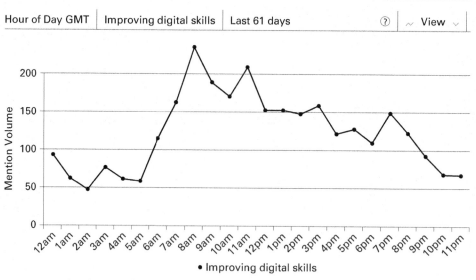

SOURCE: Brandwatch

The dogma of recruitment

Over the years we have developed a well-accepted culture and process for recruitment, which I believe is responsible for much of the lack of agility inside large organizations. Recruitment takes too long until any actual 'work' starts to be done, and it is far too easy to make poor recruiting decisions. These poor recruiting decisions can be disastrous in terms of the time and resources they absorb in putting them right, they radically slow down the progress of any projects the individual is or was supposed to be involved with and they can cause huge morale damage for the individual involved as well as the surrounding team.

The accepted process I refer to, is to gather CVs, filter them, interview people and then maybe interview them again, then decide. This process is essentially testing the ability of the candidate to write a CV and to perform at a face-to-face interview under pressure. If the job is to create standardized reports and conduct face-to-face interviews, this a great recruitment process. Otherwise, it is a pretty poor indicator of how good somebody is going to be at their job.

We have even tried to make this process more scientific by adding things like tiers of interviews and scoring matrices to try to remove personal bias. This is all great, but we need to get a better feeling of how someone will really perform doing the things that their role will involve. I don't, however, think it is fair to ask people to carry out extensive unpaid tasks before joining an organization. There is a middle ground and we can see a great example from Automattic, the company behind Wordpress.

Hiring candidates without meeting them

Dave Martin was responsible for all design and growth recruitment at Automattic, and he laid out his very successful recruitment process in a blog in late 2015. You can read the blog for the full detail (link below), but I think a few things really stand out.

The Automattic recruitment process:

https://davemart.in/2015/04/22/inside-automattics-remote-hiring-process/

Recruitment as a priority

Firstly, the pre-screening of CVs is an absolute priority and Automattic's CEO was spending up to 30 per cent of his time on this. This means that recruiting the right people was truly seen as a priority and key to how the organization would grow and flourish.

Candidates treated with respect

All candidates are responded to and encouraged to reapply in the future if the fit is not right the first time round. When test projects are carried out, candidates are paid to do these. All interview stages are done in a way that allows candidates to respond in their own time and at their own pace. This generally means using Skype chat so that discussion can be asynchronous and questions answered when convenient, as there is a clear acceptance that most candidates will have existing roles and commitments.

Trials are key

All candidates are given trial projects so that both their work and communication style can be assessed. All trial projects are paid for at an hourly rate.

What is most interesting about Automattic's process is that it led to 100 per cent staff retention at the time of writing and very often no one had spoken to or met the candidates in person before recruiting them (Bort, 2016). One caveat of this process is that everyone at Automattic works remotely, so doing a remote working process makes perfect sense. It also means not speaking face to face does not matter, as they would not be doing much of that anyway. If, however, the role you are recruiting for means working in an office or speaking face to face a lot, a trial should involve these activities.

Training and learning techniques

Having delivered tens of thousands of hours of digital marketing training and running an organization that specializes in improving digital capability within organizations, I have seen and tried pretty much every approach to improving digital skills. In Table 13.1 you will find a summary of each approach and its positives and challenges. You will then find some more in-depth analysis and commentary for each approach.

Table 13.1 Summary of each approach and its positives and challenges

Approach	Description	Positives	Challenges
Classroom	Face-to-face training normally delivered over half-day and day periods.	Immersive and interactive. Lots of creative options for exercises and interaction.	Very dependent on quality of trainer and other attendees. Implementation of learning after event. Time/travel commitment.
Qualifications	Series of formalized activities and study followed by assessment and qualification award.	Good for demonstrating commitment and knowledge.	Learning vs passing assessment. Recency of content. Time commitment and potential costs.
E-learning/ Online interactive	Interactive online training.	Learn at your own pace. Cross device and location independent. Lots of interaction and tracking options.	Getting adoption from teams. Lots of low-quality suppliers.

Table 13.1 *continued*

Approach	Description	Positives	Challenges
Webinar/ Real-time online	Interactive online training in real time.	Ability to interact as well as listen/watch. Location independent.	Quality of interaction. Technology challenges.
Workshop/ Hackathon	Interactive, output focused, face-to-face sessions.	Focus on hands-on experience. Lots of interactive options.	Complex organization. Smaller maximum group size.
Conference	Series of shorter topic focused speakers and training sessions.	Networking opportunities. Range of speakers.	Training becoming sales pitches. Variable quality of speakers.
Seminar	Shorter face-to-face training session.	Short time commitment. Creative delivery options.	Travel commitment. Availability.

Informal Learning

Approach	Description	Positives	Challenges
Podcasts	Audio training.	Don't need to be in front of computer. Can be used when travelling/multitasking.	Technology adoption. Lack of easy interaction.
Video	Video training.	Suited to many people's learning styles.	Not always easy to multitask so not suited travel. Lots of low-quality content.
Blogs/ Reports	Written content.	Bite-size learning. Huge range of sources and content.	Filtering of content. Variable quality.
eBooks	Long form written content.	Topic focused and in-depth content.	Time commitment. Lack of easy filtering. Niche topics not covered.

Classroom-based digital marketing training

Face-to-face training is still the king of training options in my opinion, as it offers a range of advantages that you just cannot get elsewhere. The level of interaction available, ability to share and develop ideas and the immersive experience of face-to-face training still cannot be 100 per cent replaced by any online trading options currently available. However, the training is extremely dependent on the quality and experience of the trainer, and the experience will also be impacted by other attendees.

The digital marketing courses currently on the market generally break down into two key options. Fastracks or generalist courses intend to build a wide range of digital skills over a day or number of days. Obviously, what you can learn in a fixed period of time across a broad range of topics will be limited, but we have seen excellent results from one- to five-day courses. The most popular options are two- and three-day courses but these represent a significant time commitment.

Deep dive courses are focused on a particular topic and allow you to develop more in-depth skills. My general advice on these is to look for delivery by a practitioner. No end of theory can come close to hands-on experience and you will learn from their hard-earned skills. Also, look for courses that have clearly defined outcomes and takeaways, as this will make it more likely you will actually implement things when you get back to work.

The biggest challenges of face-to-face learning are the time commitments and costs. As well as these fairly obvious challenges you probably also need to think about how often the course material is updated and how you will stay up to date after the session. In reality, no one training solution is perfect and you need to combine them effectively to improve skills and then stay up to date. We talk about this approach of mixing training solutions in the final section of this chapter covering blended learning.

Digital marketing qualifications

There are an increasing number of qualifications options available, but be very careful. Although higher education organizations and official institutes can deliver officially accredited qualifications, there are a huge number of organizations offering their own 'accredited' courses. Many of these courses are only accredited by the organizations themselves, and offer no guarantee of the quality of the course.

In reality, there are also challenges to the well-established educational organizations. The way that many academic and official institutes work is not well suited to the fast-moving world of digital marketing, and some qualifications and accreditations are hopelessly out of date. However, some of the smarter organizations have partnered with real-world practitioners to help solve this problem.

Another key consideration is why have you chosen to study for a qualification rather than undertake other forms of training. The key answer is generally for recognition and having something that you can put on your CV/résumé and that will demonstrate your knowledge and commitment to learning. This is perfectly valid, but you need to be wary of the learning versus just trying to pass the course. Because of the time pressure we experience when studying for a qualification, our key focus is often just passing, and this can be at the cost of learning effectively. Very often, qualifications are best followed up with a personalized, ongoing blended learning plan.

E-learning/online interactive training

Interactive online training aims to teach you skills in your own time in an interactive way that is easily digestible and helps you track your own progress. There is a problem though, and a pretty fundamental one. Most e-learning is terrible! Owing to the fact that it is often used to deliver training that is repeated again and again, it ends up being used for topics like health and safety, that most people don't find very interesting (sorry to those of you who do!) and it is produced badly. It can be too long, dull and an awful lot of what is currently available is pretty patronizing in tone.

It is absolutely possible to deliver excellent e-learning but it needs to be easily digestible, interactive, easy to understand and help you to track your own learning. The other challenge of e-learning is that custom e-learning can be expensive to produce and take a long time to get to market. Make sure you are clear on production costs and timescales if you go down the custom content route.

Webinar/real-time online training

Online webinars can work really well, and can work for very large groups, but realistically, attendees' attention levels are not where they would be in a face-to-face course. While watching a webinar, most users will be checking their e-mail and browsing social media. There are a number of techniques that can help maintain the audience's attention, such as doing regular interactive polls and questions. You can also add two-way video, which tends to focus people's minds, but the bandwidth required to do this often leads to other technical problems.

There is a wide range of platforms available from lots of different providers but many are expensive and you pay based on number of attendees. In my experience, including voiceover IP (that is, the audio is done via the internet as well as the slides) is a simpler option than requiring people to dial in via telephone as well. Although you also want a dial-in option for backup for the presenter should things go wrong.

The biggest challenge is generally the technology limitations of the webinar platform being used (or rather the speed and consistency of your internet connection that can cause these problems). If an internet connection drops out partway through a course, particularly if it is the presenter's connection, it will cause pretty severe problems! Presenting from a predefined and bandwidth-tested location is essential, and some sort of backup connection is a great idea for really important sessions.

One of the other advantages of webinars is the ability to record the sessions and use the videos as a learning resource for a group beyond those who attended the original webinar as well.

Workshops/hackathons

The aim of a hackathon is simply to carry out a workshop with the aim of completing some form of activity during the session, and have some form of output. The term originally comes from the world of software development where developers work together to generate a new piece of code, but this can equally be applied to instructor-led, and highly interactive, digital marketing workshops.

These can work internally within organizations to help people learn the skills for creating things like videos and podcasts, as well as using digital marketing analysis tools to create reports and insights.

The key challenge is having sufficiently small groups to really give the attendees enough attention in order to help them build their skills. If attending yourself, make sure group sizes are small or that there are enough instructors involved. If you are organizing make sure you resource appropriately.

Conferences

Most of us know from experience that conferences can be a hit-and-miss affair because of the quality of the speakers. Many of us will have also had the awful experience of attending what is supposed to be an informative session that ends up being a sales pitch for the company giving the session. In my opinion this is much like going onto social media and demanding that people buy your product. It just doesn't work, it is entirely the wrong forum and will do nothing but alienate potential customers.

If you are attending a conference it is now pretty easy to Google any speakers and take a look at their previous talks on YouTube. If you do attend and want to speak to the speaker, make sure you prepare in advance. It is likely a speaker will have a queue of people keen to speak to him or her after the talk (if the speaker was any good!) and it is hard for them to give everyone time when others are jostling for attention. My advice is to present yourself briefly and provide a business card with the questions you want to ask. You can then request a response and follow-up by e-mail/social media if you don't receive a response. As a regular public speaker, I have always appreciated when people have done this and have always been happy to follow up afterwards.

If you are booking an event you *must* focus on high-quality speakers, as even a terribly organized conference can go well if the audience members feel they got value from the content. Make sure you see the person speak in person, ideally before you book, as videos are not always good at communicating how a speaker connects with an audience. Also, if you are booking speakers, make sure you arrange to film the event and get permission to use the content afterwards. You should also think about doing pre- and post-event videos, podcasts and photos to provide content for your social media feeds and other content you may be creating.

Seminars

Seminars are just short face-to-face sessions and can be organized around the working day. This means there is a smaller barrier to people signing up and attending, but bear in mind if you organize any of these type of events, people start with the best intentions, and then tend to drop out last minute due to work commitments (or the fact it is a sunny day and the pub is more appealing than your session!). In my experience a 50 per cent drop-out rate of free events is not unusual.

If you are planning on attending paid-for seminars you may experience similar problems, as many commercial organizers struggle to get enough paying customers for short events and very often end up cancelling events owing to low numbers. Some of the best short sessions are put on by the larger digital marketing service providers for free as part of their marketing efforts, and these can be well worth attending for the content and networking opportunities. Think about companies like social media monitoring services, agencies, e-mail service providers, etc, as many of these have extensive content marketing plans that include physical events.

Informal learning

The next range of learning techniques are what we would describe as 'informal' learning. Informal learning refers to the various sources of content we can access that help keep us up to date and informed of the latest trends, tools and market insights. We will also look at some specific tools that can help us filter and select the best content.

Podcasts

From a learning perspective, podcasts are fantastic as people listen for extended periods of time (generally at least 30 minutes) and don't listen when sitting in front of their computer, but rather on a mobile device when travelling. This lends itself to a particular learning environment you don't really get anywhere else.

There are many places you can find educational podcasts, but the iTunes Podcasts app is a great place to start for Apple users, and take a look at Stitcher radio whatever platform you are on. You can also create internal podcasts (just an audio file) and host on your own intranet fairly easily using sound-editing software.

Video

Video learning is a fantastic option as it suits the learning style of many people who find it hard to absorb new knowledge via reading content. However, it has its own challenges from both a learner's and a provider's point of view. First of all, for a learner looking for quality content around digital marketing, finding the good stuff can be tricky. One of the disadvantages of YouTube is the sheer volume of educational content, and much of it is not great. Once you find a good video provider, make sure you subscribe to their channel so you always find their content again in the future. The other disadvantage of using YouTube for learning content is that you cannot download content for later viewing (although the new YouTube Red allows you to do just that, but it is currently available only in a limited number of countries).

Another great source of video content for digital marketing knowledge is the video provider by the major service providers. People like Adobe, Moz and Google provide a whole range of educational video content that you see via YouTube, but you can also download from their websites for later viewing in many cases as well. You will notice that Moz offer the videos from their annual conference for sale, to allow people who could not attend in person to still get value from the content. Even those videos are not cheap; I download them every year and they are some of the most valuable forms of learning I have come across.

If you are looking to create video to help upskill your team, YouTube is a good place to start and you may find our Guide to Creating a YouTube Channel useful.

Blogs

The explosion of content marketing has led to a truly huge amount of blog content, and much like everything online, the quality is variable. My advice for using blogs effectively for learning is to use a filtering tool that will bring all of the most relevant blog posts into one place where you can read them all without having to jump from one blog to the next. My favourite tool for doing this filtering and proving an interface to read all your blogs in one place is feedly.com.

Another very easy way of staying up to date with key blogs and industry news is to use Twitter for that purpose. I follow around 200 digital marketing influencers and bloggers, and their tweets point me to their latest blog posts and news. If you are already using Twitter for other purposes or you want to group the accounts you follow on Twitter, you can use the Twitter Lists functionality. Using Twitter is a simple way of staying up to date, and allows you to dip in and out of the latest news when it suits you.

e-books

There is no shortage of digital marketing books, but one of the major problems with using these books for improving digital marketing skills is how the publishing industry works. Most books take at least six months from being written to being published. Six months is an eternity in digital marketing terms, and much of the detail can become out of date. However, publishing time for e-books is getting better and many very good authors are also self-publishing, so take a look at those Amazon reviews and get reading.

The other challenge is that books are not bite-size, but they do suit different ways of learning. They are also excellent for learning in different environments, but they do require commitment. One technique that I have seen work well is to have a form of educational book club. Agree with a group of people, maybe even online, to read a particular book or book chapter, and then get together to discuss and debate your understanding.

Blended learning – bringing it all together

As we have seen there are many different approaches to improving and keeping digital skills up to date, whether for you or your team. However, no one approach will do all things for all people. For this reason the idea of 'blended learning' is very important. Blended learning is the idea of using a range of different learning formats and styles to suit each of your learners, and match the practicalities of their learning environment and organizational challenges.

The key to building an effective digital culture is building feeling that ongoing learning is part of everyone's role, not something that is supplementary or optional. For this reason, integration of ongoing learning should be built into regular processes. For example, weekly or monthly progress meetings should always include the topic of learning and knowledge sharing. The human resources (HR) review process should have clear criteria that mean that all staff must demonstrate their commitment to ongoing learning in order to pass their reviews.

Gamification in learning

Simply put, gamification refers to the use of gameplay elements in a non-game format. At its simplest, the use of things like leader boards is an effective form of gamification for training. These leader boards show which individuals or teams have completed the most training in comparison to other teams or individuals. One point to note here is that the completion of training is great, but we should also look at how much of that training has been put into practice, so we could also create a leader board for the individual/team with the most experiments in action (see earlier in the chapter for more about the idea of workplace experiments). A range of other simple techniques we can use to encourage the level of ongoing learning within our organizations is detailed below.

The progression strand

Of all the game elements used for gamified marketing applications, the most prevalent strand is the graphic representation of progression towards a goal, whether that is points accrued in a loyalty card app, or profile completion progress bars on platforms like LinkedIn. In each case, a gamified representation of the customer's journey towards a goal is used to encourage the customer to fulfil criteria that will also satisfy the marketer's conversion goals. While demonstrably ingenious, this technique is nothing new – loyalty tokens were gamifying marketing as early as the 1700s, in a physical format. These progression strands can be used within learning environments to show progression towards annual goals or to achieve things such as 'certification' where an individual or team is recognized as achieving a certain standard or level of effort.

Celebrating engagement

Identifying ways to reward and celebrate the users who engage with your learning platforms is a great first step in effecting an achievable, light gamification. *The Guardian* newspaper encourages high-quality, in-depth debate on their articles by pinning selected comments – marked 'Guardian Pick' to the top of the comments section under each article. Digital marketing experts Moz encourage their users to get engaged with their community by awarding 'Moz Points', redeemable against a range of benefits from free product trials to MozCon conference tickets.

Rewards schemes

Another gamification technique with relatively low development requirements is the digital representation of reward scheme progress. To make this work in practice, all you need to do is deliver a tally of reward points (or a comparable metric for progress) to a dedicated section of the user's profile, attractively presented against the context of the rewards the user can unlock by reaching a certain level. The easiest way to deliver the data needed to calculate reward points is by feeding data from a learning management system to the relevant user's account.

Conclusions

Getting, and keeping, the right skills and talent within your organization, will be essential to its success. An effective digital culture needs a well-thought-through recruitment process that avoids the dogma of traditional recruitment. We need a range of learning techniques to be readily available, and usage of these learning opportunities to be highly encouraged with techniques like gamification. It also needs a culture that expects and encourages experimentation with new ideas, techniques and tools, so that learning is transferred into business practice as standard.

Perspective: Growing Right – Balancing Expansion with Culture

Author: Will McInnes
Organization: Brandwatch
Industry: Social Monitoring/Data Analysis
Location: Global
Staff: 300

As we continue to grow at record pace, we are often confronted with some interesting hurdles.

One of our biggest challenges we have at the moment is finding enough great people quickly enough.

It is probably the single biggest constraint we have to growing Brandwatch.

Finding brilliant people takes time.

Maybe 3 months from scoping out the role and writing the role description to then finding the right candidates. Add to that a further 2 weeks (USA) to 3 months (senior person, Europe) of notice period.

So 3.5 months to possibly 6 months! One to two business quarters. Ooof!

That's horribly slow when you have a year to double in size.

And when your marketplace is evolving week by week, as ours has been over the past 6 months, it doesn't feel like we have this time.

Nested within this challenge is a more subtle, dangerous challenge: compromising.

Not hiring people with the right cultural fit. Or who are good enough, rather than really great. Hands on deck rather than people who take the company forward.

I face this challenge weekly and I know my many colleagues hiring do too. We currently have 40 open positions across three countries and five offices.

Those are just the ones we've managed to publish, and some of those we may hire multiple people within.

It's so important that our CEO Giles is actually making it one of his main priorities to drive this.

The pressure is on to grow, to increase our speed of development and the scope of our activities. As a team, it's what we all want.

But it's when we start compromising that we start failing (except there will be a lag – a lag that deceives us temporarily).

Airbnb wrote a great 'Don't f*ck up the culture' piece that is a helpful reminder, but we all know the story of companies that lost this along the way from first- or close second-hand experience. So it is just a reminder.

We need to look to organizations that have scaled a special culture – companies like Gore, HCL, Zappos and John Lewis that I wrote about in Culture Shock, and the others that come to mind when you think of this. (NB: writing about it – easy; doing it – hard!).

In a curious way, we have to be really long term in an environment where most things feel short term.

Personally, I really like the mantra of 'hire slowly, fire quickly', which can raise eyebrows, but it's really about doing what's right for the group, which is ultimately also best for the individuals.

A second challenge is located in this 'growing fast' domain, which is how best to scale the organizational structure and the incumbent managers.

On the structure piece, I was reading some of our Glassdoor reviews, and one of the Pros that was coming through was the flat structure at Brandwatch.

How do we 'stay flat' as we build management, as we deepen focuses on areas that were previously part of a role to now being a dedicated role or even a team?

And with our incumbent managers, how do people like me and my peers evolve ourselves and our behaviours to perform in a world we are moving from being managers of teams to being managers of managers of teams?

What does this transition from 'player' to 'coach to 'GM' to 'commissioner' mean for communication, for style, for reporting, for control and influence?

Of course, it means changing. Changing personally. That's really hard. And not everyone will want to do it or be capable of doing it.

▶

In fact, re-reading all of this I realize that this was exactly what Lee Bryant was talking about at Meaning 2013 when he put forward the delicious idea that start-ups are actually more professional than big companies, and that it's when they start trying to be 'professional' that things go wrong.

Being on the inside of all of this rather than consulting from the outside has been so interesting and actually fun to work with these demands.

My colleague Tim rather marvellously summed up how it feels:

Figure 13.6 Tim Misson from Brandwatch sums up working in a technology start-up

CASE STUDY   Team composition and recruitment in a digital world

The make-up of marketing teams, and the challenges organizations face in recruiting them, has changed dramatically over the last 5–10 years. With a perspective from an organization in the midst of a seismic transformation of its business to compete more effectively in a digital world, Dominic Grounsell, Global Marketing Director at FX and payments giant Travelex, explains more in this guest article.

If you look over the last seven or eight years, the composition of marketing teams has changed significantly, and it's needed to. These days, we need a balance of people. We need the traditional marketing skills, the generalists and the conceptual thinkers that we've always had. But we also need hard skills. Today we need people who can cope with data, people who live and breathe analytics, people who can understand technology and the complexity of digital channels. And those people have got backgrounds that are different to traditional marketers. They're engineers, they're scientists, they're mathematicians, they're computer scientists and those people often don't see marketing as a desirable career path.

I don't think we've sold our industry to these people particularly well over the years. From an outsider's perspective looking in, we look like an advertising function. What's more, we don't court people with these skillsets in university, and we don't tend to emphasize the contribution those kinds of people can make to marketing because too many of the heavyweights in the marketing industry stand up and deride data. They talk about how data is killing creativity which, again, creates this perception that marketing is actually only about creating advertising, and if you're not from a creative pedigree, you're a second class citizen. And this is really annoying, because it's not true.

As a result, it's hard to hire people with the diverse backgrounds we now need.

When you look at marketing teams today, the balance between generalists and specialists has almost reversed. Years ago, most people I met as a marketer were what you'd class as generalists. You'd have a few people who focused on direct marketing, maybe a few in advertising, and some PR specialists. Everybody else was a generalist. These days, I see far fewer people with broad, general marketing capabilities. I'm hiring more SEO specialists, SEM specialists and PR specialists, but far fewer people who are well-rounded, broad marketing managers.

This helps people in my sort of role to execute in the short-to-medium term, but it's challenging in the longer term because succession planning and leadership development becomes much harder from within. You've got to find the specialist who has the potential to be a generalist and coach them and give them development opportunities which take them out of their specialty and their comfort zone.

People like that are much harder to hire because they're in a minority, and they're an attractive proposition.

Beyond the composition of your typical marketing team, I also think we're witnessing a sea-change in the employment priorities of the newest generation – the iGeneration or Gen Z – to join the workforce.

These days, there appears to be an emerging contradiction in claimed versus actual behaviour among younger marketers coming into the industry. While much is made of the desire among Millennials to work for companies with a clear brand mission and vision, my observation is that a large number of new marketers are actually more focused on building an interesting personal career 'portfolio'.

We're seeing people more interested in the tasks and the projects they'll be exposed to than our business itself, because fundamentally – at the risk of making a rather sweeping generalization – they're focused on doing the most interesting and cool stuff possible. And that doesn't necessarily mean cool stuff for Travelex, they'll move to do it somewhere else if the timing, the offer, and other prevailing conditions are right. This is something which is increasingly being referred to as 'fluid careers', where people are drawn to project-based roles or actively try to work across a range of roles and sectors across a very short period of time rather than building a career track within one organization or sector.

Having ambitions to do cool marketing is great, but from a recruiting perspective, these shifts in mindset make the task of finding and securing good quality digital talent 10 times harder. And that's before we think about how to retain them.

In addition to the challenges presented by attracting the right talent and the rise of portfolio careers, there's also a growing trend of entrepreneurialism among this group.

The explosion of new tech products and the growth of businesses like Amazon Web Services have seemingly made it easy for anyone to develop the next big app or digital business. As a result, many young high potential people are looking at big business and asking, 'why do I need you?'. With so much excitement and opportunity buzzing around the tech scene, it's hard for bigger, more corporate businesses to compete for attention. Coding and product management have become the aspirational roles and the top talent know that they can afford to be picky on where they choose to work. In an increasingly digital world, they know that we need them more than they need us.

Strategic positioning

14

The core concept of strategic positioning is very simple, it is incredibly important to every aspect of your organization and proper implementation can be challenging. The core concept is simply: what is it that your organization stands for? What is the core purpose of your organization beyond your commercial objectives? How does everything your organization does provide value?

Strategic positioning can also be referred to as brand positioning, brand strategy, brand purpose or unique value proposition, and there are plenty of subtly different interpretations of what each means. None of this particularly matters. What we need to define is what our organization stands for and why this matters.

Bridging the gap

Our strategic positioning allows us to bridge the gap between what we want to say to our target audience, which is generally 'buy our stuff' or 'do this thing', and what our target audience is actually interested in engaging with. We achieve this through building insights-driven strategic positioning (Figure 14.1). That is, we understand our target audiences, what motivates them and therefore how we can go about providing value.

Figure 14.1 Strategic positioning helps us bridge the gap between what we want to communicate and what our target audience wants to engage with

WHAT THE BRAND WANTS TO TELL PEOPLE

BRIDGING THE GAP WITH INSIGHTS-DRIVEN STRATEGY

WHAT TARGET AUDIENCES WANT TO ENGAGE WITH

Strategic positioning in practice

Remember that your strategic positioning is not a strapline, but it should be able to be communicated simply in a sentence or two and it explains how you provide value beyond simply talking about your products or services. It is then used to guide every single interaction you have with any internal or external audiences. Let's take a look at some examples:

Table 14.1 Examples of strategic positioning for a range of different organization types

What's being sold	Strategic positioning
Online digital marketing courses	Practical and hands-on digital marketing advice
Sportswear	Helping everyone achieve their athletic potential
B2B engineering product	Market-leading knowledge and advice
Professional body	Helping you make the most of your career
Poverty charity	Make a practical difference in people's lives

All of the strategic positioning statements work because they do three key things. They encompass what we actually provide as a product or service, they give us things we can talk about beyond our product/service and they inform what we should consider at every interaction point we have.

Business-to-business service

If I want you to buy a complicated B2B service from me I need to do a number of things, but most of all I need to give you the content you need to help you make a decision. This means I need to map out all of the stages of the buying cycle you will go through and make sure all of the different questions you need answered are covered. In most B2B situations, the potential customers will not engage directly with a potential supplier until they have decided exactly what they want.

This may mean educating audiences on some topics even before they fully understand what I am offering. If this is an item that has a long buying cycle or is a very occasional purchase, I will also need to engage with the audience when they are not actually in the process of buying yet. This means I must provide value beyond just talking about my solutions.

A standard strategic positioning approach here is to position ourselves as thought leaders on an industry topic and provide value through content. This could be anything from industry news, thought leadership articles through to in-depth reports, but the key thing is I am providing value outside of just talking about what I do.

Consumer Packaged Goods

Many Consumer Packaged Goods (CPG) are things like groceries and toiletries and are generally not highly differentiated. That is, many CPG are not all that different from their competitors' products, so our positioning is very much what helps differentiate them. In fact, this is the market in which strategic positioning has been used for a very long time in the form of branding (however, branding doesn't always take into account every aspect of an organization, as we will explore more in a moment. The problem in a digital world is why would I speak and engage online about detergent or confectionery?

This is where good strategic positioning can bridge the gap between what a consumer wants to engage with and what an organization wants to talk about. By broadening the conversation and understanding our positioning, we can find topics that a user will engage with. This could be the ethical nature of our brand for a brand like Lush or our focus on natural beauty for a brand like Dove.

Complex consumer product

When we are buying a more complex consumer product, like a car or a technology product, the process is actually very similar to the B2B process, even though that product may be purchased online.

Potential customers need to understand the market and options available to them. We need to understand where they are in the buying cycle in order to provide the right content and we may need to try to engage with them before they are even considering purchase in order to build awareness and likelihood of purchase. Many complex consumer products have similar strategic positioning (although it may be communicated in very different ways) and this is normally around the areas of quality and reliability (which in turn is very similar to the thought leadership approach taken by many B2B organizations. Since these types of brands all want to communicate very similar messages (think BMW versus Mercedes or Sony versus Panasonic), they quite often don't have clearly differentiated strategic positioning.

Charity funding

When a charity is seeking donations and potentially a long-term commitment to monthly donations, engagement is essential. It is essential so I feel motivated to donate initially, but also so that I do not decide to stop donating and cancel my payment at some point.

Understanding motivations for donating become essential and working out the value exchange that is going on can be very powerful. Social media allows for powerful personal connections, and by allowing individuals to portray themselves to their peers as they would like to be perceived, the charity can use its strategic positioning to provide great value for its audience. That is, the charity can provide the mechanism via social media that makes the donors look generous, caring or any other characteristic they would like to be associated with. Charities' strategic positioning is generally related to being the most effective at supporting the cause they stand for, but since many charities exist to help a particular cause, any focus can help differentiation. For example, being the oldest and most reliable charity or being a charity that focuses on practical outcomes are all valid approaches to strategic positioning.

Beyond communications

These ideas for strategic positioning make sense from a communications point of view, but we need to go beyond this to make sure they are an intrinsic part of our digital culture. They need to be delivered not only via our external marketing, but also to give our staff and any other partners clarity on who we are as an organization. We also need to make sure that our strategic positioning is delivered at every interaction point.

Delivery at every interaction point is what makes a brand truly live its strategic positioning and helps build an overall culture within an organization. If we claim to be an ethical company because we give a percentage of our income to charity, but we treat our suppliers badly, we are not a truly ethical organization. If we put across a message of inclusiveness and equality in our external communications, but have an all-male board, we are not living up to our strategic positioning. If we claim to be thought leaders in a market, but write nothing but low-value blog content, we are not delivering our strategic positioning at all.

Content marketing and the user journey

This strategic positioning allows us to provide value at every stage of the user journey, not just when we are directly discussing our products and services, but at every interaction point we have with all of our potential audiences. These audiences are also not just limited to customers and potential customers, but also to all of our staff, as well as any external audience such as the press and industry influencers.

This strategic positioning therefore allows us to plan and implement effective content-based marketing as, once we understand this positioning, it will inform the type of content and the tone that we use to deliver that content. We also need to consider how we deliver this strategic positioning at each stage of the user journey.

Any online journey goes through a number of different stages, starting with a lack of awareness about a topic all the way though to direct commercial intent and post-purchase loyalty (or lack of!). There is a wide range of different models that can help us visualize this, but I think considering a traditional sales funnel is a great place to start.

Traditional sales funnel

A traditional sales funnel sees our target audience move from no commercial intent and general browsing or having a vague notion on a topic, through to having an active interest, on to the actual point of purchase and finally into the potential loyalty stage.

Figure 14.2 shows that this journey is not necessarily a linear one. I may spend an extended period of time browsing and revisiting content before I ever move on to the active interest phase. Also, the duration of the active interest phase will vary according to product/service offering and target audience. Once into the loyalty stage I may also find content intended for the browsing stage useful again.

With each stage of the journey I need to understand my target audiences' objectives and motivations, and work out what content and interactions will drive them to the next stage. Having a clear view of my strategic positioning will guide this.

Figure 14.2 The sales funnel

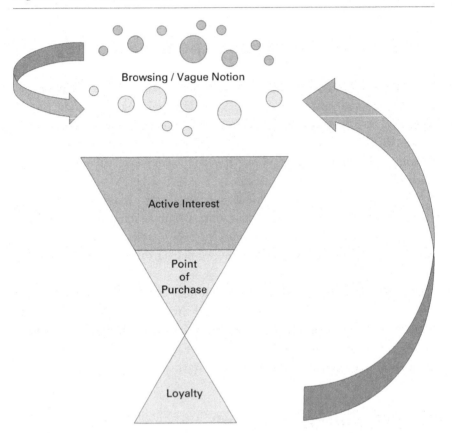

See, Think, Do, Care

Avinash Kaushik is a best-selling author, renowned analytics expert and a Digital Marketing Evangelist for Google. Through his excellent blog, 'Occam's Razor', he has described his very useful See, Think, Do, Care framework (Figure 14.3). You can read more about it at http://www. kaushik.net/avinash/, but it is a simple to understand yet very flexible and effective model for planning content.

In reality, our funnel model and the See, Think, Do, Care framework are actually telling us the same thing. We need different content in different contexts for each stage of the user journey.

Figure 14.3 Avinash Kaushik's See, Think, Do, Care framework

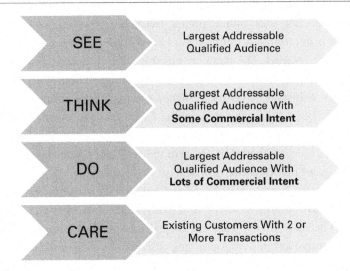

SEE — Largest Addressable Qualified Audience

THINK — Largest Addressable Qualified Audience With **Some Commercial Intent**

DO — Largest Addressable Qualified Audience With **Lots of Commercial Intent**

CARE — Existing Customers With 2 or More Transactions

Content mapping

So let's take a couple of examples and look at how we can map content against each of the stages of both user journey models. We will take two very different organizations: TargetInternet.com, a business-to-business organization that sells access to online digital marketing courses; and Tesco. com, a global online grocery retailer. Table 14.2 shows the four stages of the user journey (from both user journey models) and then shows examples of content at each stage for a particular audience.

Table 14.2 User journey models and content mapping

Stage	TargetInternet.com	Tesco.com
See (Browse)	7 top Facebook tips for social success	25 things to do with your children on a rainy day
Think (Active Interest)	Complete guide to bridging the digital marketing skills gap	20 healthy ideas for children's lunch boxes
Do (Point of Purchase)	Online digital marketing courses	Online grocery shopping
Care (Loyalty)	7 top Facebook tips for social success	25 things to do with your children on a rainy day

If we first consider what the strategic positioning of each organization is, we can see how this then informs the content planning process. Although TargetInternet.com sells online digital marketing training courses, their positioning is not 'the best online digital marketing training courses' as this is too product focused. The strategic positioning is 'practical and hands-on digital marketing advice' as this allows positive engagement with the target audiences at each stage of the user journey, not just at the point of purchase.

Although Tesco sells groceries online, their strategic positioning is not purely about being the best grocery provider, but rather about 'Every little helps' and focusing on the value and help they can provide to their customers at every stage of involvement with Tesco.

The see/browse content is of broad general interest to our target audience. The think/active interest content is actively related to what the organizations sell. The do/point of purchase is their key product offering. You will notice the content at the see/browse stage can also be used at the care/loyalty stage as well.

Authenticity

Not only is it essential that we understand our audience in order to build effective strategic positioning, it is also essential that we live that positioning throughout our organization and that we truly believe in what we stand for.

Let's take a look at an example of strategic positioning that, on initial inspection, seemed like a truly excellent idea but ultimately failed to achieve business results.

Branding for differentiation

The brand in question was Pepsi and the campaign I am referring to was the Pepsi Refresh Project. If you are based in the United States it is pretty likely you are aware of the project, but outside of the United States it didn't really get much coverage. When I heard about it and watched the case study video I fell in love. I suddenly thought that a massive brand had really got it and I was convinced initially it would be a great success. You already know it wasn't, but let's talk through the mechanics of what they did and look at what on first inspection looks like excellent strategic positioning (and in fact much of it is absolutely excellent).

Pepsi already knew that trying to differentiate on product alone was futile. Even their own video case study states very clearly that even though they taste slightly different, both Pepsi and Coke are 'brown, fizzy, soda pop'. I should mention at this time that the original description in the video was 'brown, fizzy, sugar water'! That version of the video disappeared pretty quickly.

Anyway, this was a fairly bold way of approaching things. They then went on to say that you could put your product in the hands of a superstar in a 30-second shiny Super Bowl commercial (the most expensive TV advertising slot in the world) but they were going to do something different.

To tell your customers something they clearly already knew, but that had never really been admitted, was honest and exciting. They made it clear that their product was very similar to other products on the market and that they had been marketing by using celebrity mega productions. (I was impressed, but then they blew my mind!) They said the Pepsi Refresh Project would give away the US $20 million dollars they were going to spend on their Super Bowl commercials to good causes. And that the audience could select the good causes by voting via social media. I was massively impressed, and so were a lot of other people. It gained huge coverage. It was a news story in its own right. Millions of people voted. I used it as a case study at every presentation and keynote that I did for months, and I still use it to this day.

So, with this great idea, what happened next? They ended up closing it down (quietly) and moving back to a strategy of aligning with celebrities. Why? Because it didn't generate sales. We really need to understand why.

Another viewpoint

There is a lot of analysis out there on this particular campaign, and by far the best in my opinion is that by Craig Bida on MediaPost – it is definitely worth a read:

http://www.mediapost.com/publications/article/186127/why-pepsi-canned-the-refresh-project.html

---

Authenticity

I think we can sum up why this did not work in a few words. It was not authentic. Now, I do not mean they were not donating all that cash, and I certainly do not mean that they lied in any way. What I mean is that this strategic positioning was not truly lived by every part of the organization.

There are a couple of telltale signs that really make this stand out. It was a Project. We describe it as a campaign. Both of these things generally imply that it has a beginning and an end. For this truly to have changed things, it needed to be the start of an ongoing commitment to a value proposition around making the world a better place. The thing is, we all felt that, even though this was a great project, Pepsi was not suddenly some sort of social enterprise or charitable foundation (they actually do have a charitable foundation and you can find out what good work they do in the callout box). We knew this was a marketing campaign to make us buy more soda pop. This tells us something fundamental about how strategic positioning has to be different from our traditional ideas of branding.

Authentic value proposition

We also need to be clear that your strategic positioning has to be completely authentic. If you say that you are committed to making the world a better place, you had better live by those words. If your strategic positioning says that you truly care about customer service you really had better care. Everyone in your organization needs to feel personally responsible to deliver this positioning.

Not only is the positioning important for customers, it is also important for recruiting and retaining staff. Those brands with clearly focused and ethical strategic positioning are likely to recruit better staff and retain them longer (LinkedIn, 2016).

The digital world we live in means that an organization's commitment to its strategic positioning is more transparent than ever. This transparency means that we can build powerful brands based on real promises faster than ever before. That same transparency means that a lack of authenticity will be exposed.

Let's be fair

I would like to make it clear at this stage that I really respect Pepsi for being bold enough to try the Refresh Project in the first place. I also respect their decision to can (pun intended) it when it didn't work. I do, however, feel that what they have replaced it with misses the opportunities that digital branding offers, but we will see where they go next.

And as for that charitable foundation I mentioned, you can find it at the link below, but to quote their site: 'Since 2005, PepsiCo, through its Foundation and divisions, has donated over $800 million in cash and product to qualified nonprofit agencies working in environmental, educational, civic, arts and the health and human service fields.' That is nothing to be sniffed at. Did you know about it? Neither did I. Maybe they should have focused on that....

The PepsiCo Foundation:
http://www.pepsico.com/Purpose/Global-Citizenship

Translation and communication 15

Throughout our process of interviewing digital leaders for this book, one theme stood out more than any other: communication.

You are setting out on a journey to define what your organization needs to look like to become truly digital, and then to bring about the changes needed to make that a reality. Words like transformation and change bring with them many questions, much uncertainty, and quite often nervousness and even resistance. What does this change mean for me? Will it impact how I work, or what my role will involve? What will I need to do to meet the expectations the organization has of me? How do I lead my team through this period? How involved will I be in shaping this new digital agenda or is it going to be done 'to me'? Will my influence or authority be undermined in any way and do I want to support this new agenda?

To avoid, or at least mitigate, the disruptive effects of change within your business, it is critical that you invest in well-thought-out, regular and bespoke communication throughout your organization. But communication is not just about managing the risks associated with getting your organization to do new things or in different ways. It is also about harnessing the collective ideas and energies of your workforce and channelling them in the right direction to make becoming digital a success.

Beyond the vision and the strategy and the technology, most businesses are made up of people who are central to getting things done. A strong focus on communication from the outset of your journey will underpin the kind of culture you are trying to create, and will give you a better chance of achieving your stated ambition.

Speaking the right language

One of the most basic principles of marketing is often overlooked when it comes to an internal audience: segmentation. Your business, whether you are a major international corporation or a domestic-focused small enterprise, is diverse. Just think about the different mixes of people that make up your workforce.

First, you have *different generations*. Today, you have the potentiality for five different generations in the same workforce. That is five different groups with very different personal experiences of digital technology. Some will have been born into our digital world, where the pervasiveness of technology is all they have known. Some will have been born in the 'analogue' generation, and have witnessed the pace and scale of change at first hand. How these individuals respond to the perceived threat or opportunity presented by digital has the potential to be very different.

Second, you have *different functions*. Your digital agenda will mean one thing to your HR community, another to your marketing team and something different again to customer service and operations colleagues. We talked earlier in Chapter 9 about the need to articulate what 'being digital' really means for *your* organization; it is important to take it a layer further and articulate what this means for its different constituent parts.

Third, you have *different contexts*. Not necessarily directly tied to age or tenure with your business, your people will have different personal experiences of change. Some teams, such as IT and marketing, will have been more exposed to the profound shifts in digital technology and how it affects our lives, as they have been at the forefront of understanding what it means for systems and infrastructure, and customer engagement. A more operationally focused team, such as supply chain or logistics, may have had less proximity to this.

Trying to address your total workforce with the same message and the same level of information will likely fail to resonate for most. People's questions will remain unanswered and their contributions will not be harnessed in the right direction.

What is more, those charged with leading digital transformation and efforts to create a digital culture in your business will inevitably have the most knowledge, passion and conviction behind the need for change, but you will need to make sure that this is translated for your colleagues, not pushed onto them with the assumption that they will immediately share your enthusiasm.

Structuring your conversations

When you are thinking about a particular message or story you need to convey, there is a useful way to structure your thinking so that you are translating the change requirement in a way that helps your colleagues to relate to it. We call it SIBA.

- *Story*: What is the core message you are trying to convey? What is it you need someone to understand? What is the change that you are looking to bring about?

- *Implication*: What does this mean for your audience? How will it impact their role/team and how they currently approach the task in hand? What do they need to do or do differently to support this change? And how will the business support them to play the role you need them to?

- *Benefit*: What is the benefit to the business of this change, and how does it add value to your customers?

- *Actions*: What do you want to happen after this communication? Are you asking people for their support, approval or input? Will there be an opportunity for feedback or a follow up?

Using SIBA – an example

To give an example of translating a message using the SIBA structure, let's say you are talking to your Head of Customer Service about implementing social customer support.

Story: We are seeing double-digit monthly increases in customers turning to Twitter and Facebook for support, complaint resolution and quick questions, but we are not proactively using these channels. That means we leave some customers ignored, and frustrate others by making them use other customer support channels as a second attempt. We are also damaging our reputation, because we are not part of the online conversation about our brand when things go wrong. We think there is a win–win for us if we reallocate some of our resources away from telephone- and e-mail-based support to specialize in social, and we would like to make Twitter the primary vehicle for this.

Implication: We need to reassign some of our customer service team to specialize in social customer support. This means there is a training need for some of your people, and a potential short-term resource issue as we move them away from telephone and e-mail channels.

Benefit: We think that doing this will help us to improve our overall customer service response time and satisfaction. We will be dealing with customers' issues and questions when and where they want us to, and our teams can handle more than one issue concurrently on social media, as opposed to a phone call which can only be handled sequentially. We will take back ownership of our support conversations on social media and stop issues snowballing through a lack of responsiveness. We will also help reduce the need for customers to e-mail or call with questions and support enquiries, which can be dealt with quicker through social media. This will make our customer service efforts both more efficient and effective.

Actions: We would like your feedback on this change. After we have ironed out any issues, we would like you to think about how we select the right people for this evolved role, and to work together on a transition plan so that we manage the impact on the rest of the team. We would also like to arrange a meeting for you with a business that has already undergone this change in customer service approach, so that we can draw on their learnings and ideas.

Giving your results meaning

Just as important as direction and change, is reporting on progress and performance. In keeping with our comments about the importance of translating your communications messages for different audiences, it is also particularly important to do so when it comes to reporting on progress and performance with digital initiatives and investments.

If you take the prior example of implementing social customer support, your brand team may be interested in how this impacts movement in your Net Promoter Score, but for your customer service team this may be too high-level. Talking instead about reduction in response times, proportion of questions addressed first time through social channels rather than traditional channels, or improvement in social sentiment, will be easier to link to the change you have asked that team to embrace.

While top-line metrics are valuable and should be visible to as many people as possible/practicable, it is helpful to create secondary metrics that are more meaningful to specific teams. By providing those teams directly impacted by change with an understanding of how their efforts are directly impacting performance at a more granular level will help them to see the value in their efforts. It will help to create an enthusiasm for striving to continually improve the metrics and KPIs, which they *can* influence, rather than feeling that their efforts 'somehow contribute' to a higher goal, but feeling that their efforts are subsumed in something bigger and beyond their control.

Identify the blockers

When you are having conversations around the business about your digital agenda, sometimes you will be met with overwhelming support and enthusiasm. A truly open door. In other instances, you can expect to be met with scepticism, mistrust, resistance or simple disagreement.

Finding advocates and champions for your digital transformation ambitions is important, but dealing with resistance even more so. Often, a leader or department that is resistant to change can do more to derail or block plans than a supportive leader or department can to enable them.

Being proactive early on is key. Don't wait for barriers to spring up, proactively seek out those who may be least supportive for the organization's digital agenda and take the conversation to them first, before they bring it to you. Acknowledging their concerns up front and working together to try to resolve them is likely to put you in a better position than fire-fighting.

> Find out who the decision makers are in the business that may in some way be impacted by the things that you're trying to do and/or be blockers of it. Invest disproportionately large amounts of time building relationships with those people and understanding their objectives, their points of view, their biases and their fears, so that you can manage them more effectively when you come across issues that you both face. *Dominic Grounsell, Global Marketing Director, Travelex | @DomGrounsell*

Ask yourself the following questions to help identify where you should be targeting your efforts:

- Which parts of the organization are going to be most impacted by change?
- Where is the cost of change – either financial, political, or people – going to be highest?
- Which parts of the business have been most resistant to change historically?
- Which parts of the business are the least sophisticated in their digital capability?
- Which leaders are least active on social media, such as Twitter, LinkedIn or blogging?

> If you've got a naysayer, you should really prioritize your time with them. Because my experience is if you speak to people for long enough, they'll eventually tell you why they don't like what you are proposing. And once you know this, you have a chance of changing these people around to your way of thinking, they can become your greatest advocates. Not because they go out there and tell everyone that it's a great thing, they are unlikely to do that. But suddenly when people see that those who'd been blocking something no longer are, it makes it much harder for others to block it. Because the logic is that if the

naysayers changed their point of view, there must be something positive in what you are recommending. *Simon Thompson, Global Head of Digital Commerce, HSBC PLC*

Lather, rinse, repeat

Too often, internal communication efforts have a short fuse and a big bang. What we mean by that is that they can be an afterthought to wider activities and tend to involve last-minute planning, a big launch or kick-off moment, but that they then fizzle out quickly as people return to 'business as usual' and focus on the delivery as opposed to the communication around it.

Many of us will have experienced these sorts of communication initiatives: well intentioned, but short-lived. Most of the attention focuses on the beginning of the story, but is not followed-up with reiteration of the core goal or progress updates that help people to see how your digital agenda is delivering on its stated ambitions.

When organizations set out their transformation goals, they can be met with scepticism by some, perhaps those who have change fatigue where they have been presented with visions, strategies and initiatives in the past, which have not lived up to their expectations or followed through.

In the early days of embarking on a digital transformation initiative, most of your efforts will be focused on educating people to gain common understanding, overcoming objections and scepticism, and securing buy-in to your organization's digital agenda. But once this has been achieved, or a critical mass of support reached, ongoing communication becomes incredibly important. Your focus will need to shift from securing commitment to maintaining it.

In today's world of constant change, there is no guarantee that a commitment to a project or budget today will remain tomorrow. As the demands of your business change over time, whether due to internal or external pressures, continued reinforcement of the purpose behind your digital transformation is essential to help maintain its business-critical status. Be persistent. Continually reiterate your stated ambition. Share details of quick wins, to show the art of what is possible and demonstrate where and how progress is being made.

> I think you need to engage your employees straight away to explain what you're going to try to build and then you update them month after month. And you'll see that your whole company, even though they may not have been involved in your project, will get very excited. Because everybody wants to see cool stuff.

Especially if you explain to them how useful it's going to be to the company. A few months before launching, try to ensure that your new project is seen and heard of by everyone, and that people can see how useful it can be for them in their department and their role. *Julien Callede, Co-Founder and COO, Made. com | @JulienCallede*

Understanding the psychology of change

Change is often met with resistance and can sometimes be difficult to accomplish. The 'Formula for Change' is a useful tool to help overcome resistance with three variables of change.

The formula is $D \times V \times F > R$

D is for dissatisfaction with the status quo. V is for the vision for the future desired state that you have articulated. F represents the first visible or tangible steps taken to make the change a reality. And R represents the latest resistance to change within the organization.

As you plan your digital transformation, and the communication you have with leaders or your wider workforce, ask yourself some questions with this model in mind.

Dissatisfaction: Do people recognize the need to do something differently? Are they troubled by underperformance or do they recognize a future risk to the business? If you have not got a shared recognition of the problem, you may face people questioning the need for change at all.

Vision: Have you articulated your ambition sufficiently? Have you told the story in a sufficiently compelling, motivating and relevant way to secure support?

First steps: What are the first things that people will see or hear that demonstrate the authenticity of your change ambitions? Will people be able to see, early on, that there is evidence that your vision will become a reality?

If the combination of $D \times V \times F$ is greater than the resistance to change within the organization, then your change may be possible. If you have overlooked any of these three variables of change, then it is unlikely to succeed.

The Formula for Change was created by David Gleicher in the 1960s, and subsequently refined and simplified by Kathie Dannemiller in the 1980s.

The network effect

The education and communication of your digital ambitions faces two practical hurdles: the first is time, and the second is credibility.

First, *time*. Particularly in a larger, more complex or geographically dispersed organization, one lone change agent or small team leading your digital transformation cannot hope personally to influence every stakeholder, engage with every employee, or be able to do so at every opportunity. It is simply impractical.

Second, *credibility*. Some people in your business may be sceptical about who delivers a message internally. If you happen to hail from a marketing background and are trying to engage with operations or customer support teams, for instance, they may question how well you understand the mechanics of their part of the organization, and whether you are therefore equipped to advocate making changes to it.

Leveraging the power of networks can help overcome these barriers and bring added benefits alongside. Rather than taking on the task of education, communication and reinforcement on your own, look for progressive people within the organization who show a particular enthusiasm for the potential of digital technology. Look for the people who carry sway or are respected within their departments. Identify who you could recruit to form part of a small, virtual network of ambassadors or evangelists, but don't base this on age alone – we are not saying the answer is to stick a millennial in front of people because they are 'tech savvy'!

You can work with this small team in a time-efficient way to have a much wider impact. Immerse the team members in your digital vision and ambitions. Give them the fuller picture and all of the background, not just the polished version. Work on building their knowledge and understanding of what you are trying to achieve, how it will benefit the organization and the customer, and what it means for the organization. Solicit their input into how to translate the vision for different departments, and ask for their help in identifying the implications of change across the business.

This is not about scripting or sheep-dipping. If you can secure their commitment to your plans, send them off into their departments with a mandate to bring your digital transformation to life for their colleagues. Bring them in for regular updates on issues, progress and performance, and empower them to share this in the way they feel best. Not only will you benefit from their insight, you will also have them working on your behalf in a more authentic and credible way, helping the message to permeate throughout the business.

It's a two-way street

Communication flows two ways. We are in an era where brands, content and customer communication is democratized and empowered consumers recognize that they are in control of the conversation they have with organizations. And this will be reflected in how you communicate with your workforce, as this is the context in which they live.

A truly digital business does not just preach to its people, it listens and responds. Being collaborative, as we talk about in Chapter 19, is just as important internally as it is with other members of the value chain. It is your people at the sharp end of your business who will see first hand how customers are responding to your digital initiatives and investments. It is your customer service operators, your salesforce, your logistical people. Capturing anecdotes and qualitative feedback is as important as quantifying performance through metrics and data.

What is more, the members of your workforce have their own digital lens through which they view the world. They will see what other companies are doing that might apply to yours. They will spot issues or opportunities within the business that they know well, and can contribute to how to tackle them.

When you articulate your vision for becoming a digital business, it is important to remember that your plans cannot be finished and fixed. They will evolve and adapt over time, as your external content changes, and as your business responds to your early efforts to improve your digital capability. It is important to remain open to ideas, feedback and constructive criticism – and to encourage your workforce to feed in these to you.

> We set up a company social network, using Facebook At Work. It's been running for a while now so I think it's generally seen to be pretty useful, especially so for people to engage together and share ideas. They might be crazy ideas about where to eat or what they want to see in the next collection, or who they'd like to collaborate with. And you get both really compelling answers to these questions, as well as some crazy ones. We saw that this kind of tool is actually good for motivating people, getting them to see that they can give their opinion and it will actually be listened to and acted on. *Julien Callede, Co-Founder and COO, Made.com | @JulienCallede*

- Put the mechanisms in place to enable people to get their input to you.
- Create an environment where two-way communication is not just permissible but valued.

- Incentivize and reward your people for generating ideas and suggestions that help solve business problems and improve your digital performance.
- Tell people what you do with the input you receive, and follow up.
- Spotlight successes where employee input has led to a positive outcome.

The medium, not just the message

It is not just what you say, but how you say it. Taking your vision to transform into a truly digital business to your workforce may be met with some scepticism if the medium or channels used feel a little too analogue.

Setting out your plans to digitize your operational processes, explore new digital propositions and business models, or use digital to optimize the customer experience is a great opportunity to set an example and lead from the front. An opportunity to showcase how digital technology can be leveraged to engage internally as well as externally. An opportunity to show that your organization is serious about its digital agenda and that your leaders are committed to it, and embracing it themselves as role models.

Think of how you plan to communicate with your people, the accepted norms within your business. Then challenge them – to help amplify what we have got to say, could we do this better or differently?

For example, instead of a company-wide e-mail from the CEO talking about your digital vision, maybe they should be blogging about it? Instead of leaders passively participating in all-hands meetings, maybe they should be taking live Q&As or livestreaming to colleagues wherever they are in the business or the world.

We are not advocating replacing face time and one-to-ones with all-digital communications – far from it, the power of taking the time to talk directly with people is compelling. Rather, it is about ensuring that your methods and style embody your stated digital ambitions. Digital culture is, after all, born from within.

Key points

- Recognize the differences in your workforce and tailor your message accordingly. Translate vision, strategy and performance into the context of different departments to make sure it has meaning.
- Identify those most likely to be impacted by your digital agenda, and those most likely to be barriers to change, and invest your time disproportionately in education and communication with them.

▶

- Reinforce your story at every opportunity. Do not stop communicating when you have secured initial buy-in; switch to then maintaining that commitment over time as business pressures and demands change, to ensure digital transformation remains a business-critical priority.

- Improve the efficiency and the credibility of your communications internally by building networks of employees who can evangelize your mission and act as change agents in their own teams.

- Embrace ideas, feedback and constructive criticism. Create the environment and the mechanism to tap into the collective knowledge of your workforce and reward those whose input makes a difference.

- Ensure your communication efforts reflect the stated digital ambitions you have for the business. Role-model how you would like people to communicate and collaborate and avoid the irony of pushing a digital agenda with analogue approaches.

Technology 16

Of all the areas of the digital culture framework that are the most regular cause of problems for organizations, technology is it. We will start by exploring why technology is an issue and then explore a number of options you can implement to achieve a truly effective digital culture.

Technology is often a huge frustration in many organizations, and IT is often rated as one of the top three obstacles to implementing any form of digital transformation (Fitzgerald, 2016). So why is technology such a huge stumbling point for many organizations and why does it matter?

Why technology matters

In a fast-changing environment with equally fast-changing customer expectations, customers expect more. I expect to be able to log into your website and app and see my previous order history, whether those orders were made online or offline. I expect to be able to get customer service by phone, e-mail and live chat. I expect that a fault on your website will be resolved very quickly. All of these are very standard expectations now, but can cause massive headaches from an implementation point of view. We will discuss why these things can be such a headache, but let's first consider why it matters. If you don't live up to these basic expectations I will very quickly take my business elsewhere. Furthermore, the organizations that can give me a fully personalized experience, that join together both my online and offline behaviour, are simply more likely to get my business and then keep it for longer (Moore, 2016).

Getting the fundamentals in place

In just a moment we will explore the idea of systems integration and achieving a fully holistic view of our target audiences through their offline and online interactions across multiple channels. However, before we even explore these reasonably complex topics, it is worth clarifying that many organizations have not even got the basics right yet. For example, 61 per cent of organizations have not yet implemented a Customer Relationship Management (CRM) that is mobile device optimized (MacDonald, 2016). What this basically means is that many organizations simply are not equipped to either attract new customers, or serve their existing ones, in the most effective way possible. This leads to things like poorly targeted e-mail campaigns, bad website experiences and ineffective customer services. This in turn leads to a lack of sales and a loss of customers over the long term. The business consequences are critical so we need an approach that will solve these issues.

Single customer view

The idea of a single customer view (SCV) is a very simple one, but can be extremely difficult to achieve (particularly in larger organizations). The idea is that we connect up the data we get from our mobile apps, websites, e-mail campaigns, social media and so on, integrate this with systems like our Customer Relationship Management (CRM) to build a complete picture of our audience, and are thus able to provide better integrated and personalized experience to our customers and potential customers (Figure 16.1).

Figure 16.1 Achieving a single customer view

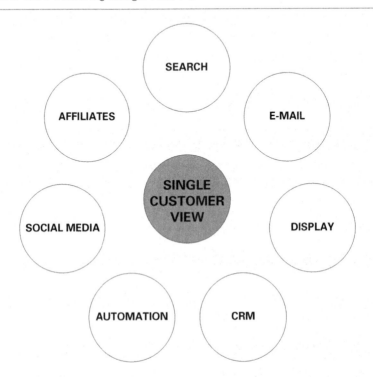

The painful truth about integration

The challenge of integrating data sources is that it is generally a fairly complicated IT project for most organizations. What we are really talking about is database, third-party supplier and legacy systems integration, and what this means in reality is complexity. However, it does not need to be this way.

If I am a small business, it is a different picture. I can get some form of web analytics like Google Analytics, a cloud-based CRM system like Salesforce, and various systems like MailChimp (an online e-mail service provider (ESP)). All of these will 'plug in' to one another with not too much effort, and I have a relatively effective single customer view.

Even in large organizations, by carefully selecting suppliers with a single customer view in mind, I can work towards this ideal scenario step by step. We may not be able to integrate all data immediately, but this should be our long-term objective.

Next step: Marketing automation

Marketing automation is something that is most often used in the B2B world, but it can be applied to almost any industry, product or service to some extent. The core principle is that if I have insight into your behaviour on a single or multiple channel, I can automatically trigger relevant communications to you at the right time.

At its most simple level, imagine getting a push notification via an app some time after you have made a purchase, asking for a review. This is a basic form of marketing automation.

At its more advanced level I can start to 'score' your behaviour across multiple platforms to try to identify particular types of customer, potential leads or customers who are having problems finding the right information.

The B2B world tends to be well suited to marketing automation owing to the long sales times, involved buying process, multiple touch points before purchase and high value of a sale. It can also be applied to consumer goods if tied in with digital services that are there to bolster value proposition. For example, a sportswear manufacturer can track your behaviour through an app that monitors your fitness goals and triggers relevant communications at the right time.

Why technology is a challenge

So, it should be abundantly clear why we need effective technology, but if it is so business critical, why is it not an issue that most organizations are addressing, and addressing quickly?

Lack of leadership

Many organizations lack senior leadership prioritization of technology-related issues and they are lacking a clear vision of how technology can be used to advance the business.

Lack of urgency

Very often, although the need for technology improvements are recognized, they are seen as critical enough to create the level of urgency required to overcome the various challenges that need to be addressed. Also, in already successful organizations, the need to implement any large-scale technology projects is often seen as an unnecessary challenge.

Legacy systems

Existing technology that needs to be replaced or integrated with new systems can add additional complexity and cost to implementing new systems.

Resistance

A distrust of new technologies and how much they are actually required can create an atmosphere of cynicism. This is particularly damaging when these attitudes are held by any level of management within an organization.

Pace of change

Because technologies can become outdated so quickly, the fear of any new project being superseded before it has even been fully implemented very often results in implementation paralysis. The fear of wasting resources implementing a new system that will quickly be out of date means that no projects are ever started.

Lack of measurement

Starting from a point where the impact of existing systems is not being measured makes it very hard to justify the implementation of new systems.

ROI-based arguments are normally the most effective at getting buy-in across an organization for new technology projects.

Internal politics

Changes in organizational structure, new technology capability and new ways of measuring activity all have an impact on people's roles. These changes can lead to individuals being concerned over a loss of influence or responsibility as well as exposing poor performance. All of these concerns lead to different forms of internal politics that can slow and stop the implementation of new technology projects.

Resourcing

Technology projects can be expensive and time-consuming, and therefore it is easy to resist committing the necessary resources, particularly when short-term objectives are prioritized over longer-term strategic goals.

Creating an effective digital culture for technology

How do we overcome this list of complex challenges? Although there is no one single solution for all organizations, those organizations that have successfully implemented complex new technology projects have a number of factors common to their approach.

Strong leadership and clear vision

Most of the challenges outlined above can be overcome by having strong leadership that can clearly communicate a strategic vision that includes the importance of improved technology. This means the first port of call for any transformation team is to get buy-in from the most senior leaders. Buy-in on its own, however, is not enough, and senior leadership must be seen to be driving and spearheading the change.

Once strong leadership and a clear vision have been established, this will minimize resistance and internal politics. Any resistance and internal politics can be managed owing to them not being aligned with the clear strategic vision for the organization.

IT as a service

Very often IT is a department that is focused on risk mitigation, rather than on enablement. This leads to a culture where IT tries to minimize anyone doing anything risky, which in turn limits capability and experimentation. We must operate in a sensible way with an awareness of risks, but not to the extent that it limits success. We therefore need IT leaders and managers who are flexible and understand the need for constant change.

One approach that transformed a very large global beauty brand, was the conversion of IT from a risk mitigation focused department into an internal service judged on customer satisfaction. In this case, however, since this is an internal service, the customers were internal members of staff who had any interaction with IT. At the end of each quarter, IT could not achieve its targets, and therefore its bonus pay, unless internal customer satisfaction was above a certain level.

This approach re-focused IT on helping to achieve other teams' goals, and led to clearer communication when challenges were faced. Rather than IT simply telling other staff 'no', 'can't be done' or 'we don't offer that', they were more likely to try to communicate the logic behind a decision. This increased communication also led to more awareness and understanding of IT issues across the organization.

Measurement-based approach

Once measurement frameworks are implemented and we know what we are measuring, why we are measuring it and how it connects to our bottom line results, it becomes much easier to justify any technology investment.

Unfortunately, we often need to invest in new technology projects to make measurement possible in the first place. For example, without an effective CRM system or well-integrated web analytics, it may not be possible to measure the outcomes of our sales or marketing efforts. This can make ROI-based arguments impossible, but this in itself should be a key argument. If we are operating in the blind in regard to ROI, even if we are having success currently, it should be a priority to implement systems so we can measure, iterate and improve our results.

Training and education

The gulf in knowledge of technology-related topics, between the teams most impacted by it, and those that are responsible for implementing projects, is often huge. For example, sales and marketing teams are often ignorant about the key technologies that can be used to make their roles more effective. Therefore, a commitment to learning about these topics is essential. This knowledge can then be used for more clearly defining requirements, analysing potential solutions and for understanding challenges in implementation.

A broader understanding of technology-related issues throughout an organization can also aid cross-team communication where technology has an impact.

Conclusions

Technology is one of the most common digital transformation-related challenges but, in reality, most of the complexities it causes can be overcome through strong leadership and vision. An effective digital culture requires openness and flexibility across the organization and a commitment to broader understanding of technology is essential.

Process and governance 17

Of all the organizations and individuals interviewed for this book, what stood out from those that had been successful in digital transformation projects was their focus on mapping processes. This focus on the processes involved allowed for repeatability, transparency, scalability and iteration. We explore an example set of processes later in this chapter, but first, let's start by exploring why processes are key to success.

Planning for a fast-moving environment means working with uncertainty. We don't know when the next new technological innovation will come along, we don't know how much traction the social network will get and we don't know when the next social media crisis will occur. This uncertainty means that unless we put processes in place to monitor, review and iterate our activities, we are passive victims of change. Processes allow us to be proactive in our approach to change.

Where we need processes

Every activity we carry out, in every area of our business, should be process mapped so we can iterate and improve it. Realistically, however, although process mapping how you reply to e-mail may allow you to improve your efficiency, we are never going to process map everything. There are, however, a number of obvious elements of your organization's activities that should be process mapped, so we can iterate and improve effectiveness. Things like our sales process, marketing activities, training approach, recruitment process, should all be mapped out so we can identify strengths and weaknesses and look at possible improvements.

These processes can also help us identify opportunities and problems early on. Mapping process around brand monitoring, social media crisis management (which we will explore in detail later in this chapter), search rankings and other constantly changing areas of our business can maximize the opportunities we identify, and minimize the impact of any negative events.

Avoiding 'bottom of the drawer' syndrome

Another key factor that differentiated those that had implemented successful digital transformations and had an ongoing commitment to an effective digital culture was the fact that their processes were actually being used. The risk of process mapping is that it is done once, and the process sits at the bottom of a drawer, or more likely on an intranet, and remains unused. The process is then quickly forgotten, aspects may be missed, and any opportunity for iteration is lost.

In order for processes to be used effectively we need a couple of simple techniques to be adopted. Firstly, a broad range of software tools is now available to allow us to work in a process-orientated way. Tools like Slack allow teams to work collaboratively, follow processes, manage task lists and integrate with a range of other tools. Many modern CRM systems like Salesforce allow us to map processes and create automatic triggers, and cue us to carry out certain activities at certain times. Modern brand monitoring tools like Brandwatch can automatically trigger alerts when mentions of particular topics change statistically significantly. All of these tools make the adoption of processes more likely.

Regular process review sessions also help keep the way we do things front of mind and allow us to iterate our processes. These can be scheduled on a quarterly or six-monthly basis to review the steps in any given process and look for opportunities for improvement. One tip for these process review sessions is to bring someone outside of the process into the session to get an objective perspective.

Workplace experimentation

Changes to processes and how we approach different activities should embrace the concept of workplace experimentation. This concept, which we touch on in a number of chapters throughout the book, is one of implementing changes as a controlled experiment to access their positive (or negative) impact. For example, if we believe a change to the sales process could improve sales but we are unsure of its overall impact, we could implement it as a controlled experiment. That could include taking a small group or an individual onto our sales team, letting them work with the new process, and seeing what impact it has on their sales results.

It is important that people understand the ethos of these experiments throughout the organization, and that no one is treated negatively when the outcome of an experiment is not a success. For example, if a salesperson does not think a sales process change is a good idea but it is then forced upon him or her, the salesperson may not implement the change completely effectively. Also, even if he or she does try to make things work, and results are not positive and sales targets are not hit, does the salesperson then fail a review and not get a bonus? It is important that those people responsible for a particular process are encouraged to be the people who are suggesting and implementing improvements to those same processes.

Internal service level agreements

Another important element of process mapping is making sure there is clear governance between teams and departments. Where one team's processes has dependencies on another part of the organization, internal service level agreements (SLA) can help clarify what is expected of each of the parties involved. A typical example would be where an organization has a compliance team. Very often communications are passed from marketing to compliance for sign-off before distribution. An internal SLA would lay out how many such signs-offs can be handled by the compliance team over what time period and in what time period they will be completed.

Effective SLAs make allowances for 'out of the ordinary' requests as well. For example, if the normal sign-off time by compliance is three days, but a social media crisis occurs and we need something turned around much more quickly, we need to define a process for these out of the ordinary requests and to whom we can escalate issues and how quickly we can expect an emergency response.

An innovative approach to these kind of quick turnaround challenges, especially when they are likely to happen on a semi-regular basis, is to use a voucher system. Normal turnaround may be three days, but each department could be given three vouchers that they can use throughout the year for getting four-hour turnaround. This means that fast turnaround can be achieved, but the demand is limited and managed for exceptional circumstances.

Example process mapping

Social media is a potentially powerful and risk-filled arena for most organizations. Because of both the opportunity and risk involved, social media activities are well suited to process mapping and planning. In the next section of this chapter we will work through the process of effectively implementing a social media policy and how this can be used to minimize and manage social media crises.

Social media crisis management – effectively implementing a social media policy

The internet is awash with social media disaster stories, and blog posts titled '10 <insert over-the-top adjective here> social media fails' are almost certain to get lots of attention online. But why do we like to see other people's disasters so much? Beyond the amusement value of some of the incredibly dumb things that people do, it is generally because the audience wants to learn how not to repeat the mistake. Figure 17.1 is a word cloud (the bigger the word, the more times it was mentioned), showing the words and phrases

Figure 17.1 Word cloud of phrases mentioned online connected to social media disasters

that were mentioned online related to social media disasters (this was created using the fantastic Brandwatch (https://www.brandwatch.com) tool, which monitors over 90 million online sources such as social platforms, blogs and news sites).

So, many of us are searching for how to manage a social crisis, but it also seems that lots of us are searching for ways to avoid these things happening in the first place. Figure 17.2 breaks this down a little further.

Figure 17.2 Words used in association with social media disasters

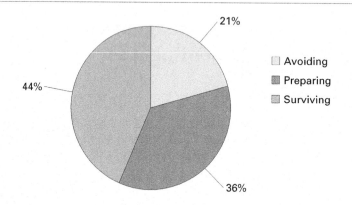

Culture and process

It is pretty clear that not only do we need to try to avoid social media disasters, but we also need a realistic view that they do happen, and no level of preparation will allow you to avoid them completely. It is important to make it clear in your organization from the outset that, although you can minimize problems occurring and you can fix them as quickly as possible by implementing the appropriate processes, you cannot avoid them happening altogether. The world is a chaotic place and no one can predict the future, but we can implement processes that deal with the most common patterns in which problems occur and processes that avoid us making most common mistakes in the first place. We also need a culture that understands that building and iterating processes are essential and accepts that complete control is impossible. Culture is an important point to mention here as well because, as we can infer from the data below, the fear of social disasters is significant. Social media managers and marketers are very concerned about the impact these disasters can have on their companies, but very importantly also on their careers. Figure 17.3 shows the number of mentions of avoiding, surviving and preparing for social media disasters, and the spikes in

Figure 17.3 Peaks in interest caused by new articles being published giving advice on the topic

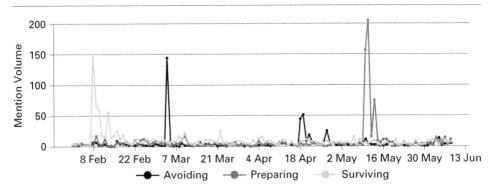

mentions are not disasters happening and getting coverage, but rather a new article being published giving some form of guidance.

How to avoid a social media disaster

They key to avoiding social media disasters is process. Below is a series of steps that should be taken to allow social media to be carried out in the most risk-mitigated way possible. For some small and agile organizations, some of these steps may be overkill, but in any large organization a 'belt and braces' approach can pay dividends in the long term. Also, always bear in mind that social media itself is not normally the cause of a social disaster; it's more often to do with customer service or product problems, so make sure these teams are involved.

Panel sign-off

Before anyone in the organization is able to start to undertake any social campaigns or activity, they must go through due diligence. This basically involves clearly documenting a series of answers to questions related to that activity. This would include, but is not necessarily limited to:

- What are the objectives of the activity?
- How will you resource the activity?
- What are the current topics of conversation in the topic area?
- What are our competitors doing in the area?

- Who are the influencers in the topic area?
- Do we have the appropriate tools in place for managing the activity?
- What happens if something goes wrong?
- What does going wrong look like?
- Have we brainstormed all of the possible disaster situations (see disaster prediction below)?
- Do we have an escalation policy and crisis management team?

It is also worth building a dialled-down version of this process into any project of any type across the organization, so we are always asking the questions 'What are the social media risks?' and 'What could go wrong?' Once these questions have been answered, they are then reviewed by representatives from relevant parts of the organization. This normally includes representatives from marketing as well as legal/compliance. If the questions are not answered satisfactorily, the proposal is not accepted and must be revised and submitted again. If they are answered satisfactorily, the proposal is accepted and the teams can go forward and implement their plan, on the condition they do it within the bounds of the social media policy. This may sound laborious, but it does have an advantage for those wanting to implement their social plans. Once they have sign-off, and as long as they adhere to the social policy, they don't need sign-off for every post, tweet or response going forward.

Social policy

Many social media policies simply list what we should not do. They are lists of rules that either live in a drawer or on an intranet and are infrequently used. Although these policies should outline things we should not do, they should also form a regularly updated guide to what we should do. By giving examples of things like tone of voice and examples of tweets that have been successful, a social media policy becomes useful and far more likely to be used.

For examples of a wide range of other organizations' policies, take a look at:

http://socialmediagovernance.com/policies/

Disaster prediction

A very simple and effective part of your social process should be a brainstorming session. Get together as many people as you can comfortably fit in a meeting room and make sure you have a mix of roles, ages and seniorities, if at all possible. Do not have too many senior people or anyone whom others will not speak freely in front of. You then ask everyone to brainstorm anything that could possibly go wrong with the social activity. Could the hashtag be hijacked and used for something else? Could the campaign be manipulated to communicate a message that was not intended? Is it just a dumb idea that people will laugh at? You need to let people be completely free to come up with pretty out-there ideas. The next stage is to filter what you have come up with. You then put the whole list to an anonymous vote, allowing people to indicate if the risks identified are possible (or simply ludicrous) and the perceived likelihood that they could happen. Any deemed to be completely unlikely are discarded. Those that remain then have responses planned for them. If someone hijacks your hashtag, what do you do? Stop using it? Respond? In each case you need a planned mechanism to either fix or contain the problem (more on this in the section on managing a crisis).

Social listening

Every social project should start with a listening project. This will allow you to understand what the popular themes of content are, who the influencers are, and should also help you to identify any potential risks. You can also look at what your competitors are up to and set some expectations of the level of engagement you would like to achieve. You will need a decent social listening/monitoring tool – we use https://www.brandwatch.com and I highly recommend it. You start by creating a set of words that you want to look at, and the better tools give you a query builder to do this. You can see an example query in Figure 17.4 that monitors a whole range of words, but also excludes some word combinations.

Staff training

All staff should be trained in your social media policy, and this should form part of your induction. They should then get updates on a regular basis to either update their knowledge or to just remind them of the key issues. This way people know what is expected of them, what they should and should not do, and what processes and tools are available.

Figure 17.4 Building a query for social media listening

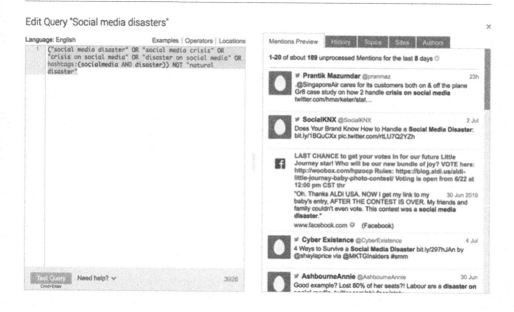

Ongoing monitoring

Once you start a campaign or any social activity, you then need ongoing social media monitoring tools. This will allow you to gauge the reaction to your efforts, monitor your competitors easily, identify influencers and, most importantly for our purposes, identify any issues very quickly. The better tools will automatically create alerts for you that flag up any change that is statistically significant without you needing to look for it (Figure 17.5).

Clear responsibilities

You need to clarify from the outset who is in charge of monitoring and reporting on social media. What happens when that person is not around? Who takes over? Who is responsible for dealing with customer complaints that come in via social media? How quickly should they be responded to? How quickly should your internal legal or compliance team turn things around? All of these activities and more need to be clearly documented and expectations for different roles and teams made clear. Very often internal Service Level Agreements (SLAs) are a good idea in large organizations, so that different departments and teams are clear on what the expectations are.

Figure 17.5 E-mail alerts for topics that are growing quickly (screenshot of Brandwatch's 'Signals' system)

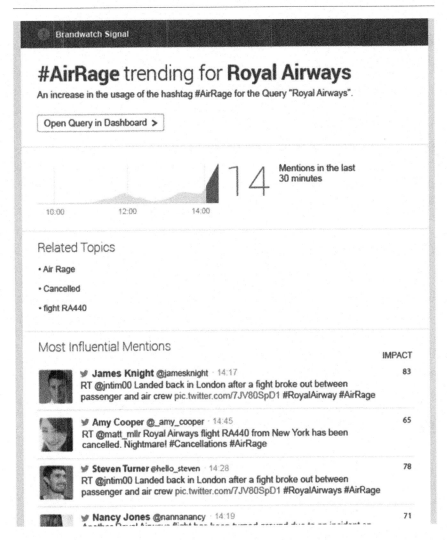

Response tracking

Once you start getting responses to your social activity, you will need to respond to many of these (whether negative or positive). The more successful you become at social media, the more of these responses you will get, and this is when you will need a tool to help you. It is important that you track things like complaints and you respond to compliments, and make sure they are assigned to the right person and tracked through to completion. There is a range of tools available but two of my favourites are Hootsuite (for managing social media) and Conversocial (for customer service at scale).

Escalation process

Once something is identified as a potential issue it is essential there are clear guidelines of what happens next. Who needs to be told? Via which channel? How quickly? It is no good sending me an e-mail on Friday afternoon if I am not checking my e-mails until Monday morning. There needs to be a clear process for flagging up potential issues to the right people, and a fall-back process for when they are not available. We also need to define what a problem looks like and who is responsible for deciding when something is becoming a problem.

Crisis management team

Once we have decided something is becoming an issue (and it is sensible to be pretty cautious in your approach; better to escalate something that blows over than ignoring something that explodes into a crisis!), we need to have a nominated crisis management team. This team will be removed from their day-to-day roles and put onto dealing with the issue head on. Therefore, we also need to plan what will happen to the team's normal workloads.

Social media crisis management plan

This is the process that should be initiated once things have been handed to the crisis management team.

Speed of response

Most social media disasters happen because organizations are paralysed by fear and a lack of planned responses. It can then take too long for a response to be signed off and things escalate. Our aim is to respond to any issue as quickly as possible in a measured way. We therefore need to answer these questions as quickly as possible:

1 Do we have any pre-planned responses from our disaster prediction process?

2 If so, are they fully suitable?

3 If so, have they been signed off for usage?

If we have no pre-planned response we need to create a response. Normally an honest and open tone is appropriate, not a corporate 'don't admit any liability' tone. Taking responsibility where an issue is our fault is desirable and suggesting a resolution. Always be cautious if the resolution will be seen as insufficient for the problem that has occurred. Best to make a gesture of goodwill than be seen as uncaring.

Once the response is created we need sign-off as soon as possible. The crisis team should have immediate access and prioritization of their requests to the person who is able to sign off the response.

Not responding

Bear in mind that sometimes no response can be the best response! If a serial complainer is complaining again, even though you responded positively previously, you may make a decision to ignore the complaint/comment. Audiences are quick to identify serial complainers and often, if you respond, you simply give them a platform from which to escalate things further. However, ignoring a complaint or comment should only be done as a conscious decision and still requires sign-off.

An alternative approach to not responding at all is to respond via a third party. For example, if we previously identified advocates, that is people who are positively inclined towards us and are likely to say positive things, we may ask them to join the conversation. Telling people what to say on your behalf can backfire, so we are simply asking them to join the conversation. Always remember, though, that an overzealous advocate can also make things worse, so it is important you trust how this individual will act.

Monitoring reaction

Once the response is issued, we need to see how the audience reacts. Very often involving advocates at this stage can also help as they can amplify and share our response. Be prepared for your response either to get no traction or fail to get the desired impact. In this case we loop back to preparing further responses and involving advocates again.

Holding patterns

Very often, particularly in large organizations or when dealing with legally sensitive issues, we cannot issue a full response immediately. In these cases it is essential to issue a holding response and to set expectations. For example, we may say that we are aware of the issue and that while we carry out some internal investigation, we cannot respond in full, but that we will issue a full response by a defined deadline. This kind of holding response can help to minimize rumour and escalation before our final response. It makes sense to always have a holding response prepared and signed off in advance so these can be issued as quickly as possible. Holding responses should be carefully crafted so they are not seen as admissions of guilt or cause any other forms of further escalation. It is worth putting your holding response through a disaster prediction process, as discussed earlier, as well.

Post crisis debrief and social policy update

Once the disaster has been averted or passed, we then need to make sure it doesn't happen again. The crisis team should debrief the relevant teams and then amend the social media policy to add additional advice and learnings. All staff should then be briefed/trained on the change.

Social crisis management conclusions

The majority of social disasters can be avoided by following a series of processes that we have identified, but bear in mind the majority of social disasters are not caused by social activity. Normally social disasters are caused by issues like customer service or product faults. Therefore the responsibility for preventing disasters lies across the organization and all staff need awareness and training.

When social disasters do occur, we need well-prepared crisis management teams and processes to minimize the damage and give a response as quickly as possible.

Conclusions

The combination of process mapping, workplace experimentation and iteration allows us to adapt to a fast-changing environment quickly and effectively in a scalable way. We need to develop a digital culture that embraces and encourages this approach, to allow the individuals that make up our organizations to work effectively.

Structure 18

Most businesses are not built with the customer in mind, let alone the modern, digitally centric world we now live in. We seem to spend much of our lives working around internal structures that make sense on paper but often create more of a challenge than they solve in a digital context.

When you are looking to transform into a truly digital business and create a digital culture that underpins this, you cannot avoid the design of your organization. It governs how people interact and communicate, where decision-making sits, and where responsibility and accountability lie.

In most organizations, internal structures are designed to avoid chaos. They typically group people by common role (function), product division or market – or a combination of the three. While these structures are efficient, they reflect a very internal view of the world.

You see, digital doesn't respect internal fiefdoms, silos, conveniences, legacies or P&Ls. It cuts across a business indiscriminately, which can mean that those charged with leading digital transformation and working on key digital projects tend to find themselves working across multiple functions, divisions and budgets, not to mention occasionally treading on toes and encountering lots of different personalities along the way.

It is not as simple as saying 'well, change the structure then'. Organization design is complex and can rarely be decided upon based on one factor or priority. Many of the reasons for the current setup of your organization will be sound (or mandated, such as for regulatory purposes). It would be both short-sighted and impractical to suggest that digital trumps all. The aim is to find ways to make your structure work for you, not the other way around.

Avoiding the digital silo

One of the first dilemmas you might face when looking at how to digitally transform your business, is how best to organize digital within the organization. Unfortunately, there is no silver bullet here – there is no universal model or design that is the best for any given scenario; it depends on lots of factors specific to your organization.

However you choose to approach your digital organization, the priority is to ensure that digital doesn't become siloed. That is not to say that it shouldn't be structured as a standalone function. Rather, whatever structure you go for, it doesn't create the impression that 'digital happens over there', or give people ammunition to say 'that's the digital team's problem'.

Technology doesn't respect silos. Customers do not respect silos. Digital cannot be siloed. Becoming a truly digital business and evolving your culture to support that is a challenge and priority for your whole organization. The trick is to find the right ways of working an organization design model, without building barriers or distancing your digital leaders and people from the wider business.

To truly become a digital business and to avoid digital becoming a silo, it has to be part of a continual process, it needs to be a fluid part of your business plan. When I arrived at City AM, it was very siloed. As a media owner, we had a print team and a knowledge gap around digital. Our print team would naturally be focused on the newspaper and were not equipped to efficiently sell digital solutions. And vice versa. It's not important to me where the revenue comes from, what's important is providing holistic solutions, and the right solutions, for our advertising partners. I don't care what platform it is, which means now, with digital training in place, it gives them an open ticket to sell cross platform. Our executives need to be experts in every single one of those mediums. Now our commercial teams' responsibilities and incentives are targeted across all platforms, rather than focusing just on one. *Charles Yardley, Chief Operating Officer, City AM*

Digital and organization design: common approaches

Let's explore some of the ways in which businesses are approaching where digital sits within their organization design. There are several common approaches, each with different pros and cons.

First is digital as *a standalone function*. Here, a single department brings together all of the digital expertise and people within the business. Typically, these functions exclude back-end IT infrastructure and systems, instead focusing on digital capabilities and initiatives which directly impact the customer, such as CRM, digital communications channels (including social media), user experience and front-end web design, and digitization. In this scenario, the digital function provides an internal service, for instance supporting marketing campaigns, as well as implementing new systems, such as marketing automation or digital customer support.

Second is digital as *a centre of excellence*. Here, digital teams (or those involved in using or managing digital channels) are dispersed across an organization, for instance in product or marketing teams, but a small digital function is formed to provide specialist expertise or niche skills where needed, to create best practices and to advise other teams on leveraging digital to maximum effect for their part of the business. In this scenario, the centre of excellence typically doesn't have authority and sign-off on what another part of the business decides to do, and doesn't control their budgets; instead, they operate on an 'influence and engage' basis. This approach is particularly common in diverse and matrix-style organizations, such as professional services or banking.

Third is digital as *an internal change agency*. Here, a digital team is formed to help accelerate transformation, rather than replace or augment how digital is currently approached by a business. Typically, this digital team will be small, with deep and specialist expertise, and will be assigned to key business problems or opportunities, acting as internal consultants and change agents. Think of it like deploying a taskforce: they get in, diagnose the problem, define the solution, implement it, then get out.

Structure is an enabler, not a solution

Changing organizational structure is often seen as something of a panacea, and not just for digital. If an organization wants to effect change, moving people's reporting lines, locations and teams is often an early consideration. And why not? If we want certain teams to collaborate more, let's put them under the same division or leadership. It seems logical.

Unfortunately, restructures frequently tend to disappoint. According to recent research from McKinsey & Company, less than 25 per cent of organization redesign efforts succeed; 44 per cent run out of steam after getting under way, while a third fail to meet objectives or improve performance after implementation (Aronowitz *et al*, 2015).

In reality, what looks good on paper often doesn't translate into something happening on the ground. Simply relining people on an organization chart will not necessarily mean that they will collaborate better or make something happen faster, or whatever the goal is.

Too often, the structural design is the main area of focus. Who to put together, who to separate, and who should lead what. It also often gets very political, as power bases and perceptions of influence become affected, often resulting in a great idea for change being watered down to what is ultimately politically acceptable and palatable for senior leaders.

In our experience, changing structure to support your digital ambitions can be positive for an organization, but only if structural design and organograms come second to developing a clear understanding of strategy, objectives, processes, ways of working and talent priorities. In essence, figure out exactly what needs to happen and how, then design the best structure to enable that.

Ask yourself: why are you thinking of changing your organizational design to support your digital ambitions? Fundamentally, you need your people and teams to do new or different things in new or different ways. Are they failing to do so at the moment because they have got the wrong reporting lines or sit in the wrong building, or because they do not fully understand what they need to do or how they need to do it? It is more likely to be the latter, which means focusing on solving those questions, communicating and training people. Then you can change where they sit or report, with a better chance of success.

Find your operating rhythm

There are few, if any, digital endeavours within a business that can be implemented by one individual in isolation. From diagnosing a problem and developing a strategy to solve it, to execution and go live (be that internal or in-market), most of what you will need to achieve as you pursue your digital ambitions will involve other people and probably other teams.

That means you are going to be dependent on others to make your digital transformation a success, however you try to use structure to mitigate that. And that is where your organization's operating rhythm comes into play.

An operating rhythm helps to get different people and teams to communicate and interact in a defined and consistent way, centred around common objectives or priorities. This is not another term for an internal comms plan – this is about institutionalizing a set of 'routines' that ensure the flow of digital projects is not interrupted.

As you are working on new digital initiatives that need input, support or delivery from multiple stakeholders, establishing a clear routine that ensures information flows around the right people, at the right time, can help avoid hitting delays, blockages and breakdown in communication. This can include project milestones, progress reports, issue resolution, KPI reviews and knowledge sharing.

To identify how your operating rhythm could be improved, ask yourself the following questions in relation to your key upcoming digital projects:

- Who are the key stakeholders involved in making this project a success?
- What role do they play? Who provides input, who supports, who approves and who has delivery responsibilities?
- What information needs sharing among this group and when?
- How does information, communication and interaction among these different stakeholders happen today and how can we streamline that?
- What is the most efficient way of sharing information and communicating as a group on a regular basis?
- Are you using digital technology to maximum effect to enable this?

Break down walls

Organization design, when done well, should help to enable the free flow of information and communication around an organization, yet in many instances it often does more to establish or reinforce internal borders and boundaries than overcome them. Just ask yourself a few simple questions:

- Do you have regular, meaningful exchanges with other functions in your business?
- Do you use cross-functional project teams and working groups to maximum effect?
- How well do you really understand the mechanics of other departments?
- Do you understand the priorities and pressures facing other functions in your business?
- Could you do more to learn from and share with other teams around your business that support or deliver your organization's customer experience?

Most of us, if we are honest, would probably score ourselves with a 5 out of 10 on the above questions – 'good intentions, but could do better'. In the pursuit of clarity and accountability, structure and organization design separates out processes, tasks, activities and people within a business into clusters, and that separation can easily lead to siloed working.

While structure exists for good reasons, it is important not to let the boundaries between departments and teams become too pronounced, particularly given the pervasive nature of digital technology.

To avoid this, we think it is healthy to proactively break down the walls that exist within your organization. Find ways to improve your understanding of how different teams operate; the pressures they are facing and where they are stemming from; the insight they have into customer behaviour and expectations; and their impact on the customer experience. Do this on an ongoing basis, not just when embarking on change or transformation initiatives, and make sure it happens below just leadership or management levels.

Here are a few practical ways of breaking down walls – and remember, it is a two-way street. It is as much about you learning about other functions as it is them learning about yours:

- Pair up key people across different teams, on a form of 'buddy' system.

- Set up shadowing opportunities with various departments, where you will spend a little time observing and understanding what they do and how they do it.

- Run monthly 'lunch and learn' sessions where you invite guest speakers from other teams to share insights into their department, or update on key projects, etc.

- Formalize this process with secondments (typically one, three or six months) or job swaps, where you despatch a team member to work in another department for a set period, actually *doing* a role, not just observing it, then bring him or her back to the original team with deeper cross-functional understanding.

- Have representatives from your team attend key monthly team meetings in other departments, and invite representatives from other teams to sit in on yours.

Do you need a Chief Digital Officer?

The last few years have seen the emergence of a new position within the C-suite: the Chief Digital Officer. Indeed, we interviewed a number of people in such positions during our research for this book.

It joins the growing list of 'C' level appointments that industry commentators and publications tend to clamour for when something becomes a disruptive or industry-wide issue. Recent examples include, among others, calls for a Chief Data Officer, to address the growing importance of big data, analytics and accompanying privacy and legislative issues; a Chief Diversity Officer, to address organizational imbalances in talent profiles and the consequences of a lack of gender and ethnic diversity at senior leadership levels;

and a Chief Customer Officer, to bring ownership of the total customer experience under one executive leadership position.

The question of who should lead a digital transformation is one that many organizations struggle with. Should it be the CIO (Chief Information Officer) or CTO (Chief Technology Officer), given their technology expertise? Or should it be the CMO (Chief Marketing Officer), given his or her experience with digital channels and proximity to the customer? Should the CEO be the ultimate sponsor of digital given his or her organization-wide remit? Or does digital transformation and culture change need a dedicated leader at senior management level, to provide deep expertise and elevate it from a single functional area?

In reality, there is no one right answer for every organization, but there are some key considerations to help determine whether a Chief Digital Officer (or Digital Director, or similar) is right for your business:

- Is there an urgency behind your digital agenda, for instance due to competitor activity, an industry disruption or falling commercial performance?
- Does your current leadership team have the capacity and capability to lead a digital transformation initiative?
- Is your current organizational structure too siloed to have digital led by one single function?
- Do you need challenging at a leadership level by someone with credibility, deep digital expertise and a truly 'digital first' mindset?
- Do you need to make a strong statement of your digital ambitions and signal to internal and external stakeholders your commitment to transformation with an executive-level appointment?
- Has your business recognized the need for wholesale change and transformation, rather than just incremental change?
- Does your business need a catalyst who can stimulate change across a business that is perhaps currently unwilling or resistant to it?

If you do decide to appoint someone at executive level to lead your digital transformation, it is worth recognizing that this may well be a short-term or transitional role. Ultimately, the aim of a transformation and change programme is to embed a capability so that it becomes business as usual, rather than needing to be an initiative. Once all corners of your organization have fully embraced digital technology, the need for a Chief Digital Officer should diminish, as digital becomes the norm for your business.

Key points

- Avoid digital becoming a silo. Find the right ways of working an organization design model, without building barriers or distancing your digital leaders and people from the wider business.

- First develop a clear understanding of strategy, objectives, processes, ways of working and talent priorities, then let structure follow. Figure out exactly what needs to happen and how, then design the best structure to enable that.

- Find your ideal operating rhythm – define how you want different people and teams to communicate and interact, centred around common objectives or priorities, institutionalizing a set of 'routines' that ensure the flow of digital projects is not interrupted.

- Break down walls – find ways to improve your understanding of how different teams operate; the pressures they are facing and where they are stemming from; the insight they have into customer behaviour and expectations; and their impact on the customer experience.

- Ask if you need a Chief Digital Officer to support your transformation. Is there an urgency or commercial imperative; a lack of leadership capacity or capability; a need for challenge at leadership level; a need to signal commitment to change; too much of a silo mentality between functions; a recognition of the need for wholesale change; and a need for a catalyst to overcome resistance to change?

Connections 19

When you are working to bring about change in your business, it is easy to get lost in the complexities and challenges of your own organization, and lose touch with the outside world.

Businesses all over the planet are grappling with the same fundamental challenges and opportunities as you are. What does digital mean for our business? How do we adapt to changing customer behaviours? Where will the next disruption come from? Which trends should we be watching and what should we be paying most attention to?

We live in a networked world, where it is easier than ever before to connect and collaborate with others. If you are looking to embrace change and influence the digital agenda in your organization, remember that you are not alone, you do not need to have all the answers, and you certainly do not need to reinvent the wheel!

Key to building a digital culture is embracing the idea of being connected. It means building meaningful and productive networks; partnering with other members of the value chain; seeking insight from and sharing learning with customers, peers and industry bodies; and seeking out help and good practice from media owners and those at the forefront of digital change.

Curate your own stream

One of the challenges of the information age we live in, is that there is just so much noise out there it can be hard to know what to listen to. Fortunately, technology doesn't just provide the dilemma, it can help provide the solution.

There are three practical things you can do, leveraging platforms you are most likely already using and already familiar with, to help you to cut through the noise, the clutter and the purported expertise, and tap into the insight and thinking of those who can really help build your 'digital IQ'.

First is *Twitter lists*. Depending on how you use Twitter, your timeline can often feel like a strange mash-up of personal things (celebrities you like, music artists you follow, cooking channels you find useful, etc) and professional things (businesses you admire, thought leaders you look up to and competitors you keep an eye on). Creating custom lists enables you to filter your timeline into discrete topics or groups of people.

Second is *LinkedIn influencers and publishers*. While LinkedIn's origins may have been in recruitment and building networks of people you work with, over the last few years it has shifted into being a content platform, enabling brands and individuals to publish thought leadership and content, sharing it with the growing reach of LinkedIn's community. As well as those people you are connected to (your '1st connections'), you can also follow individuals, companies and topics to enrich your timeline with content and thinking from beyond your personal network.

Third is *content aggregators*. Rather than visiting dozens (or even hundreds) of different news websites, blogs and apps, content aggregator apps like Flipboard, Feedly and Apple News aggregate a personalized newsfeed just for you. Depending on which platform you prefer, you can customize your feed and follow publishers, businesses and topics, all brought into one place.

We have probably all sent ourselves a link to a website to look at later, downloaded a report and never gone back to it, or printed out an article that has got lost on our desks. In today's always-on, time-poor world, we often struggle to find the time to explore outside thinking and ideas, but taking these three practical steps can help to make it easier to keep a finger on the pulse. These tools have been around for a while and some of us have even tried to use them for this purpose previously – it is definitely worth trying/revisiting as not keeping up with change is no longer an option.

Who to follow

Your ideal list will be specific to your business, your market context and your digital agenda, but there are several categories to think about when seeking out who to follow:

- leading digital agencies, such as DigitasLBi, AKQA and SapientNitro;
- management consultancies with strong digital research and thought leadership capabilities, such as CapGemini, Accenture Interactive and Deloitte;
- industry commentators, such as Tom Goodwin at Havas Media, David Edelman at McKinsey & Company, Dave Chaffey at SmartInsights and Andrew Grill at IBM (and, of course, our very own Daniel Rowles at Target Internet!);

- academic institutions leading digital research, such as the MIT Centre for Digital Business;
- industry and trade bodies that conduct research and education on digital, such as CIM, IAB, ISBA and E-Consultancy;
- media publications with a strong editorial focus on digital, such as *Harvard Business Review, McKinsey Quarterly, Marketing Week, Campaign, Quartz, Fast Company* and Raconteur reports for *The Times*.

Unlock the value chain

It is not just your business that is grappling with the changing digital landscape, or sizing up opportunities to use digital technologies to improve performance. If you look at the ecosystem in which your organization exists, you will find others facing the same or similar context to you, and there is a great opportunity for collaboration, or knowledge sharing at the very least.

Think about the range of different organizations operating within your value chain. You have suppliers and vendors whose core role may be helping you to run your operations. Partners and resellers who help deliver your proposition to market. Agency partners working alongside your marketing teams but also supporting other businesses in different markets. Major customers, also facing the challenges of digital disruption both in how they interact with your business as well as how they manage their own. And even competitors, where there may be commercial value in 'coopetition', while remaining fiercely competitive in other areas.

There are several practical ways in which you can create a productive dialogue with businesses in these groups to explore digitization and digital transformation, for mutual benefit:

- Knowledge sharing: set up regular workshops or meetings to share experiences, progress and learnings.
- Formal collaborations: identify common areas where combining teams to tackle a digital challenge can yield benefits while drawing on less resource from each party (for example, retailers and manufacturers collaborating on research into changing customer behaviour patterns).
- Commercial partnerships: identify projects where funding and resourcing can be shared by more than one party, and both parties benefit from the product development or process improvement investment (for example, digitizing operational processes such as invoicing).

The benefits of collaboration with the value chain

Establishing these sorts of opportunities brings a number of potential benefits for your business.

First, *increasing the talent pool*. By drawing on expertise from outside your organization, you will be able to bring new talent, ideas and experience to bear on your business challenges, without facing the costs of employing consultancies or hiring new staff.

Second, *reducing risk*. Pooling resources, whether people or financial, can help you to reduce the risks and uncertainty associated with new investments or initiatives that are otherwise unproven.

Third, *strengthening relationships*. Whether with suppliers, partners or major customers, working together to try to improve digital capability and performance for mutual benefit can help build closer ties and embed relationships with strategically important organizations.

Fourth, *not repeating mistakes*. Learning from other businesses can help you to avoid costly mistakes (whether in time or financial terms) and take advantage of good practices and successes from other businesses.

And lastly, *improving pace*. Combining intellect and experience across one or more organizations can help speed up your ability to interpret and diagnose issues, and develop your plans for how to tackle them.

Build your network

It may seem a statement of the obvious, or even somewhat facile, to suggest that social networking is an important contributor to building a digital culture. Platforms like Twitter, LinkedIn, Facebook, Xing and WhatsApp have become somewhat ubiquitous in our lives, yet many of us remain passive users at best, perhaps overwhelmed by the sheer scale of people and information that interact in these platforms.

If we are honest with ourselves, most of us could probably do more to use these tools to build meaningful professional networks, sweat those networks to make sure we are both giving and receiving value, and connecting the virtual world with the real world.

As we have previously discussed, you are not alone in trying to understand how your organization can compete effectively in a digital world. Beyond colleagues and counterparts across your organization, we have already touched on the latent potential within the wider value chain. But outside of those people and businesses you can readily interact with millions of other professionals that social media tools, such as those mentioned above, can help you to connect with.

Start small. Ask your co-workers a bit more about their professional history and connections. Who do they know that there could be value in you talking to or meeting? Can they help introduce you to other people from their network that could add value to the digital agenda you are working on?

Look for other versions of yourself. Be proactive and look for people with a common job title and context to your own. Seek out others who may be a more distant connection and reach out. A coffee, a phone call, a meet and greet. You will be surprised how many people are receptive to help, advice, sharing, or just a bit of old-fashioned camaraderie.

Revisit your existing network. When was the last time you went back through your LinkedIn connections? More than 60 per cent of LinkedIn users have more than 300 first-degree connections (Statista, 2016), but can you remember everyone you have linked with after meeting at a conference or accepted a request from after a meeting? When is the last time you actually spoke or wrote to some of your LinkedIn connections and asked to talk? It is worth carving out some time to revisit who you don't know that you know, recalling why and how you connected, and identifying people it would be helpful to reach out to. After all, that is why we use LinkedIn, and why we send and accept requests in the first place.

Get out more

We are all busy, aren't we? The pervasiveness of mobile devices and connectivity has fuelled an always-on culture, both at home and at work. For many, the concept of a 9–5 working pattern has been eroded as evening and weekend e-mails have become the norm, even to the extent that the French Government recently tabled legislation to make such working practices illegal (Mosbergen, 2016).

There is a wealth of opportunities to 'plug-in' to the latest thinking in digital through conferences, events, forums, networking groups and membership communities, yet these activities are now seen as far more discretionary and extra-curricular than in prior years.

Ultimately, we are all personally responsible for our own professional development and it is incumbent on us as individuals to assign these learning opportunities with a higher priority (and for those of us who lead and manage others, to set the expectation that this is important, not a 'nice to have').

To say that 'getting out more' is an important contributor to creating a digital culture, while accurate, is perhaps a little trite. Nonetheless, external-izing yourself (and encouraging the same of your peers and team) is essential to ensure you are attuned to the fast pace of change in digital technology. This doesn't have to mean planning a schedule of external engagements that become more burdensome than useful.

First, *do not over-commit*. Try breaking it down into quarterly schedule of opportunities to get out of your comfort zone and day-to-day operating role, and assigning a level of priority for the various conferences, events and similar that you identify. Pick one external activity a month that is critical and must be attended. Have a further two or three that would be ideal to make if prevailing conditions allow, and then have a tertiary set of 'nice to have' opportunities, which you can judge case-by-case as to whether you have got the capacity to attend or participate.

Second, *set clear goals*. Why are you attending? What do you want to gain from your time spent and how is this relevant to your current priorities? What do you need to leave a particular event, conference, roundtable or workshop having achieved? Is it about making new connections, talking to someone in particular or answering a particular question?

Third, *how will you transfer this back to your business*? What will you do the day after your external event? What do you need to act on or write up? How will you share this with colleagues or your wider team? What feedback do you want on your takeaways? Do you need to plan a follow-on internally to discuss or take action on your experience?

- Where are the key conferences and events tackling digital developments, culture change and digital transformation that align with the digital agenda and priorities we have as a business?

- What networking groups and communities exist that I could join, to both contribute and take away ideas, insights and learnings for my organization?

- What membership communities exist that tackle the questions we are facing as a business, and how do I get access to these?

- In the absence of externally arranged events and meetings, could I pull together some shared learning opportunities among my peers within and/ or outside of my sector?

Seek out the innovators

The United Kingdom, in common with a number of other countries, has been witness to significant growth in start-ups and entrepreneurial networks in recent years. The digital economy is booming, and an ever more attractive employment prospect to the digitally native Generation Z.

In the United Kingdom alone, there are copious examples of entrepreneurial organizations that either have digital at the core of their business model (such as Made.com), have leveraged digital technology to great effect to build their brands and innovate their customer experiences (such as Cambridge Satchel Company), or are using digital to disrupt established industries (such as ASOS.com or Atom Bank).

Start-ups and entrepreneurial organizations have something of an allure to bigger or older players. They are not bogged down by bureaucracy or hampered by governance and overbearing processes, and they seem to be able to operate at a pace and with an ability to pivot that many established organizations could only dream of. They are also able to attract younger digital talent in ways that frustrate larger, less 'sexy' organizations (see the guest article in Chapter 13 from Dominic Grounsell, Global Marketing Director at payments giant Travelex, for more on this).

While it is impractical to suggest that a large, established or legacy business could or should reinvent itself as a Silicon Valley-esque business, there is a lot that you can learn from these organizations, and they are often very open to sharing and collaboration – and there are two practical things you can do to tap into this digitally native community and bring learnings back into your organization.

Get out there. See some start-ups, some incubators, see what's happening in the digital community. All too often people get lost internally and lose a connection with the fast-changing outside world. *Russ Shaw, Founder, Tech London Advocates | @RussShaw1*

Accessing the start-up community

Once you are clear on your digital agenda, and the priorities you have for digital culture change, try to identify players in the start-up scene who are doing interesting things either on the periphery of or adjacent to your market. Or look for those in completely different sectors who are using digital technology in smart ways to address the issues you are facing. Or simply identify businesses whose ethos, culture or business model is interesting to you, and who you would like to learn more about.

For instance, if you could spend some time with the founders or employees of digitally rooted organizations and start-up disruptors such as Made.com, Atom Bank, Uber or Deliveroo, what would you ask them? Would it be interesting to understand how they manage talent in the face of constant change? What could you learn from their approach to agile project management? What insight could you draw from their test-and-learn methodologies? What transferable ideas could you take from how they nurture and sustain their culture during rapid growth and expansion?

It may sound somewhat clichéd to suggest 'hanging out' in Shoreditch will contribute to building a digital culture, but the principle of immersion and exposure can be helpful. There are a number of hubs forming both in the United Kingdom and beyond, where you will find concentrations of technology start-ups, digital entrepreneurs and incubators where innovation and collaboration is second nature.

Shortlist some interesting businesses or individuals you would like to meet who are relevant to your digital agenda. Write down half a dozen questions you would like to discuss with them. Give yourself a target of trying – either on your own or, ideally, with others from your organization – to have at least one meeting every month or two. Then reach out – pick up the phone, send an e-mail, or contact them through social networks such as LinkedIn or Twitter. Failing that, reach out to some of the digital networks formed to help this community connect, such as Tech London Advocates or Central Working.

Digital 'labs' and open innovation

Many large, established and legacy businesses have recognized that their setup, business model and culture can be a barrier to attracting the kind of digital talent they need. They have also recognized that 'hiring in' is only one of the resourcing options at their disposal and that there are opportunities for more collaborative approaches.

In recent years, a number of organizations across sectors have begun to approach digital experimentation on more of an open innovation basis. Rather than competing for talent that may not be attracted to a corporate environment, or taking on all of the risk associated with new digital tools and technologies, these organizations have instead created 'labs' where they invite third parties to collaborate with corporate teams to look at business challenges and solve problems. In return, they offer these early-stage start-ups support and resources, ranging from working space to financing, to access to expertise.

Organizations such as Tesco, Allianz, Coca-Cola and Barclays have all created labs to draw external expertise to bear on the challenges and opportunities they face in areas such as technology, big data, social media.

While open innovation is part of the answer, rather than the answer in itself, it could help your business to accelerate efforts to tap into the pace, expertise and agility that start-ups and entrepreneurs have to offer, free from the restrictions and bureaucracy that often typifies larger, more cumbersome corporates.

Key points

- Keep your finger on the pulse with latest thinking, ideas and insights on new and emerging digital developments by identifying key individuals and organizations to follow, and use social media tools to curate a personalized information stream that cuts through the noise.

- Explore ways to share and collaborate with suppliers, partners, major customers and even competitors to increase your access to talent, reduce risk, strengthen relationships, learn from others' mistakes and improve pace.

- Take a more proactive approach to building and getting value from your professional network. Start small by asking colleagues for introductions to their contacts, seek out people in similar roles and contexts as yourself and revisit your existing professional network to identify opportunities to re-establish dialogue and sharing with contacts from your past.

- Take personal responsibility for creating and protecting the time for external learning opportunities, both for yourself and for your team, if relevant. Make attending and participating in external events more manageable by setting three-month plans and prioritizing the essential, the ideal and the 'nice-to-have'. Set goals for each activity and determine how you will codify your take-outs and transfer this back into your business.

- Seek out start-ups, entrepreneurs and incubators to learn from those at the forefront of digital innovation and the very embodiment of digital culture. Identify people and businesses that are relevant to your digital agenda and proactively make contact. Explore whether open innovation and labs or incubators could be a way for you to fast-track bringing new digital innovations and collaborations into your organization.

Measurement   20

In order to effectively implement a number of elements of our digital culture, we need effective measurement techniques and frameworks to be in place. For example, building an iterative approach to our processes is generally impossible unless we can effectively measure their impact on our desired outcomes. We also cannot implement a culture of innovation without the ability to measure the results of these innovations. In numerous places throughout this book we have also introduced the concept of workplace experimentation, the idea of running small iterative tests of new techniques, tools and approaches. This experimentation is futile without the ability to measure the impacts of our efforts.

To meet these measurement requirements, we need an effective measurement framework that allows us to test small elements of our tactical activity and see what impact they have on our overarching business objectives. This chapter outlines a complete framework for measurement, with a focus on sales and marketing activities, which can be implemented across our organizations. This framework allows for the key areas of digital transformation to be implemented and for the ongoing application of our digital culture to be developed.

Digital strategy and measurement in perspective

One of the greatest and most commonly made mistakes in digital marketing and sales activity generally is not setting campaign objectives that can be easily measured. The next most common mistake is not setting objectives that can easily be connected back to business objectives. This means we cannot judge the success of our campaigns and therefore it becomes impossible to calculate ROI and justify our digital marketing budgets.

The following measurement framework can be used to help shape and deliver our digital strategy as well as helping to plan and measure tactical campaigns and calculate ROI.

Setting primary objectives

In order to measure the success of any digital campaign we need to start by deciding what we want people to actually do online. Fill in a form, buy a product, download a report or watch a video, for example. Our primary objective is the closest thing we can get people to do online to our end business objective (however, this may still be some way from our end business objective). The easiest way to understand this is using a few examples.

Business to business

Our end business objective is a sale of our product or service, but in most cases what we want from our websites is leads. A lead is someone filling in a form or picking up the phone and calling.

Consumer brand

Our end business objective is somebody walking into a store or using an online store to buy our product. We may not own that store or website. In this case my primary objective is engagement with content to build awareness and a desire for that product.

E-commerce

Our end business objective is a sale online and our primary objective is a sale online so there is no difference between the two objectives.

Web analytics packages

Throughout this chapter we will be exploring how we can use web analytics to help us plan and implement our digital measurement frameworks. Google Analytics, the free analytics tool from Google, has more than 83 per cent global share of the analytics market (Web Technology Surveys, 2016) and we have therefore focused on this package throughout this chapter. It is entirely possible to implement this framework using any other web analytics package. For example, Adobe Site Catalyst, the other market leading package, has equivalent reports for all of those highlighted here in Google Analytics.

Setting primary objectives as analytics goals

By understanding what our primary objective is we can then set this up as a goal in our web analytics. This means we have a direct measure of the success of any digital activity we are carrying out. It is fundamental at this stage to understand the different type of analytics goals and work out how to set these up properly (Figure 20.1).

Figure 20.1 Different primary objectives require the selection of different goal types. Screenshot of Google Analytics goals

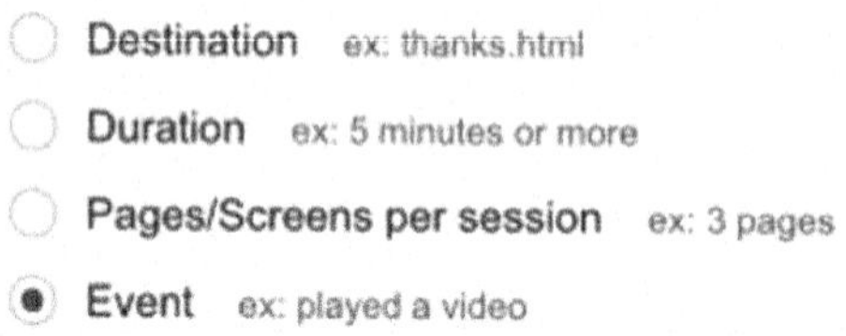

- ○ **Destination** ex: thanks.html
- ○ **Duration** ex: 5 minutes or more
- ○ **Pages/Screens per session** ex: 3 pages
- ● **Event** ex: played a video

Destination

The most commonly used type of goal and easiest to set up is a destination goal. A destination goal simply measures someone on our website getting to a particular page, and generally speaking, this will be a 'thank you' page. This could be the page that says 'Thank you for filling in our form', 'Thank you for completing the online purchase' or any other number of different pages that confirm an action has been carried out. By someone getting to this page we know he or she has completed our desired action and can therefore record it as a goal.

Duration

This type of goal measures visitors to our site who stay for longer than a defined duration of time. This could indicate engagement with our content, but always remember, it could also indicate users who are finding it difficult to complete their desired task and it is taking a long time. We may use this type of goal when our primary objective is content engagement, but event goals can often be better for this.

Pages per session

This type of goal measures visitors to our website who look at a certain number of pages (or more). Again this could indicate engagement with our content but it could also indicate people on our website trawling through lots of pages and being unable to find the content they were looking for. You may use this type of goal when our primary objective is content engagement, but again event goals can often be better for this.

Event

This is the most commonly used type of goal when we are trying to judge engagement with content as a primary goal. Where as a destination goal looks at pages loading, event goals look at something happening within that page, such as the page scrolling down, a play button being pressed on a video or somebody playing a game on a page for five minutes. The downside to event goals is that they need additional code added to web pages, but this is fully documented and can easily be set up by a web developer, agency or freelancer.

Connecting primary objectives to business objectives

You may be looking at this so far and seeing some potential problems. How do we know that people filling in a form actually leads to business sales? That is the next thing we need to consider as we start to build our model.

An enquiry form being filled in is not a sale, and somebody engaging with our content does not mean he or she is going to buy anything. Therefore our model needs to consider this and we need a way to bridge the gap (where this exists) between business objectives and primary objectives (Figure 20.2).

Figure 20.2 Connecting business objectives and primary objectives

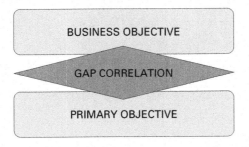

Thankfully this is relatively easy to do in most cases and we will revisit this in more depth later.

Digital channels driving primary objectives

The next stage in developing our model is to look at how each channel is driving these primary objectives and what we need to measure for each of these channels. We can now add in digital channels to our model and define the things we measure for these channels as our indicators for each channel. The key indicator for each channel will be how much traffic that channel drives to our website, but we will also have a number of other indicators depending on the channel. These indicators are all things we could try to improve that will in turn lead to more traffic from the particular channel coming to our website (Figure 20.3).

Figure 20.3 Adding digital channel measures to the framework

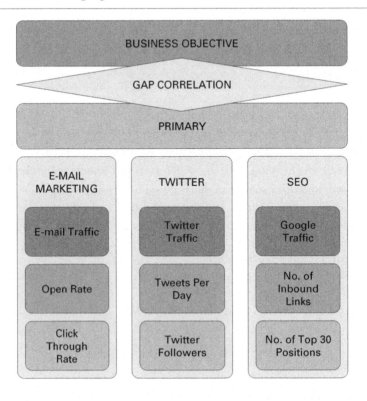

So, for example, we can see for the E-mail Marketing channel, our key indicator is the volume of traffic driven to the site from e-mail marketing. However, we will also be measuring our Open Rate and Click Through Rate as these are things we could improve in order to drive more traffic to our website from this channel. It should also be noted that indicators are not limited to having three measures per channel and we would probably also measure the size of our e-mail list here as well.

Organization-wide tracking conventions

In order to track some sources of traffic through to your website you will need to use tracking code. Tracking code is simply text that is added to a web link in a format defined by the analytics package. Then, when the traffic source is shown within your analytics package, the details you have entered will be shown. Let's walk through an example to make sense of this.

If I place a link in my e-mail that drives traffic to my website without adding tracking code, the traffic from the e-mail will show up as direct traffic. The reason for this is when a user clicks on a link in an e-mail, Google doesn't generally know where that click has come from (unless we are talking about web mail). Therefore to really understand our e-mail visitors we need to add tracking code to all of our links so we can separate where the traffic has come from and analyse it properly.

So let's explore this a little further to understand why this is more than just a small tactical consideration. In any large organization, there may be many different tactical activities across multiple channels for one particular season, event or campaign. For example, if I am a large supermarket and I have many different Christmas-focused activities, across social media, e-mail, paid search and display advertising, I may want to answer the question 'How are our Christmas campaigns contributing towards our end objectives?'. Without consistent tracking code across all these channels, it is not an easy question to answer. I need to look at the results from numerous channels and try to filter out any non-Christmas activity as well as look at how the channels have worked together. By using consistent tracking code, I can simply apply filters to my analytics to bring all of these activities under a single grouping.

▶

When we say that we need 'consistent' tracking code, this simply means using the same naming conventions across the organization. This means there must be a resource where anyone across the organization can look up the appropriate naming convention for a particular event, campaign, season, etc.

Generating traffic code is very straightforward and thankfully Google gives us a tool to simplify things. First of all, just search 'Google URL Builder'. You will then find the Google URL builder (which is just an online form for generating tracking code). You enter the page you want to link to, fill in a couple of fields and it will generate a new link for you that includes your original link and appends the tracking code. Now, if you add this to your e-mail, when somebody clicks on the link, it will be reported in Google Analytics as 'campaign traffic' along with the name you gave it and any other details entered into the URL builder. The only problem with this form is that it allows free text entry for campaign names, etc, so can very easily lead to inconsistent naming conventions. Owing to the simple structure of URL tracking codes, we could simply create a spreadsheet that gives a dropdown for things like campaign names, thus eradicating inconsistency across the organization.

Understanding how digital channels contribute

You may have noticed something else that is missing from our framework at this stage. Just because we drive more traffic from a digital channel, whether that is Twitter or e-mail or anything else, it doesn't mean that traffic will convert into our primary objectives being completed. In fact it would be relatively easy to gain lots of followers on Twitter, drive lots of traffic to our site and see no primary objective completed (because it was the wrong audience). Therefore we need to build a contribution score into our model that tells us how much that channel has contributed towards our primary goals being completed. Thankfully, because we have set up our primary objectives as analytics goals, there is a Google Analytics report that does this for us very easily.

Multi-Channel Funnels Report (MCF)

MCF report shows us, of all the people who completed our analytics goals, which channels they used on the way there (and it can look at this over a period of time, up to 90 days currently). Understanding what this is telling us is really important, and the key point is that the channels it shows are not the last thing somebody did before completing our goal, but **one** of the things that person did. This is important because a journey through to completing a primary goal may include visiting the website many times and coming in from lots of different places. The report provides a contribution percentage so we can understand how each channel (or group of channels) is contributing towards the goals being completed (Figure 20.4).

Having this information means that we can now add a contribution percentage to our measurement framework. This means we can then measure, not just how much traffic each channel is driving, but how much this traffic is contributing towards our primary objectives (Figure 20.5).

This contribution percentage can be taken directly from our MCF report and allows us to look at how effective a particular channel is, but also to look at how this impacts the overall picture of contribution and how channels are interacting together.

Gap correlation

One of the final steps in developing our measurement framework is to revisit the potential gap between primary objectives and business objectives and try to understand how we can bridge this gap. Essentially there are three potential scenarios that we need to consider.

E-commerce

There is no gap as primary and business objective are the same thing.

Lead/enquiry generation

Our primary objective is somebody filling in a form, so we need to track these through to potential sale. This can be done using most Customer Relationship Management (CRM) systems, and CRM systems like Salesforce are geared up to do this easily.

Figure 20.4 Google Analytics Multi-Channel Funnels in action

Multi-Channel Conversion Visualizer

See the percentage of conversion paths that included combinations of the channels below. Select up to four channels.

Organic Search & Direct & Referral & Social Network: 2.88% (9)

Channel	% of total conversions
○ Organic Search	48.72%
○ Direct	41.03%
● Referral	32.05%
● Social Network	9.94%

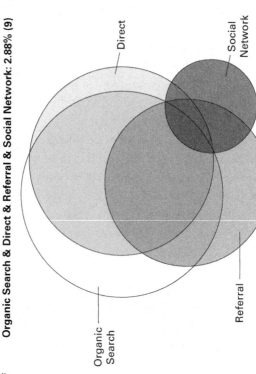

The overlap areas of the circles above are approximations.

Figure 20.5 Measurement framework with channel contribution added

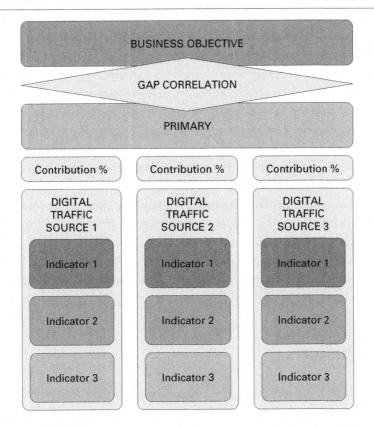

Branding

The primary objective here is engagement with content because our business objective happens on a third-party website or physical location so we cannot track it directly. The gap here can be measured by careful use of sample surveying and questionnaires to understand the correlation between people who complete our primary objective and the people who completed our business objective. So, for example, we could add a questionnaire to our product packaging that asks customers who have purchased a product which of our media and digital channels they used before their purchase. Although not easy, this approach can help bridge gaps in our knowledge that have not been available until now.

Workplace experimentation

The final step in building our measurement framework is to start using it. We can now look at which channels seem to be contributing well or poorly to our objectives. Once we have focused on a channel we can look at which indicators we may be able to adjust in order to improve things. This will allow us to develop new tactical campaigns that may, for example, grow our e-mail list, improve our open rate, get us more Twitter followers, or improve any of our channel's indicators. Once we have done this, we can see what impact this has on the channel's contribution percentage and then continue to iterate through this process.

These opportunities for iteration can allow us to implement small workplace experiments. For example, we might try a new approach to e-mail design, try to tweet more regularly, entirely stop using a particular social channel or just try a different tone of voice in our communications. Once we have a measurement framework in place, it is possible to see the impact of our efforts.

Conclusions

Although building a measurement framework and the accompanying tools and processes is not necessarily easy, it will allow us to effectively build and measure our digital efforts and work through towards understanding the ROI for each of our channels. It also means we can implement iterative experiments to test new ideas, channels and techniques, all essential to building an effective digital culture.

Innovation and entrepreneurship 21

Very often when we think of innovation, a range of hi-tech companies comes to mind, with large research and development budgets, pushing the boundaries of technology. Companies like Apple and Samsung are renowned for a constant stream of new products with technological innovations. However, in order to implement an effective digital culture, we need to go beyond these narrow definitions of innovation. A culture of innovation means constantly looking for opportunities to improve how we do things, whether that is through the use of new technologies, tools and techniques or through the constant improvement and iteration of our existing systems and processes.

Equally, when we consider the idea of entrepreneurship, we generally think of lone business people trying new ideas and rapidly growing start-ups. The truth is that we need to embrace and nurture entrepreneurial behaviour within our organizations no matter how large their size.

The right culture, that embraces innovation and entrepreneurship, can help us to embrace the new, improve what we already do and deal with constant and fast-paced change. This chapter will explore some practical techniques we can use to implement this approach.

Culture of managed risk

At the heart of any innovation-focused culture is the ability to try out new ideas, tools and techniques quickly and easily. As the market around us changes ever more quickly, the need for the ability to test and learn as quickly as possible is essential. Although easy in principle, this test and learn approach leads to several tactical and cultural challenges. The most important starting point is to have clear communication from leadership that positively encourages experimentation and testing. Failure should not be feared or stigmatized when it comes to trying new things, and that can require a serious change in attitudes throughout an organization. This does not mean that not hitting sales targets or running expensive and ineffective marketing campaigns are suddenly going to be encouraged. What it does mean though, is that we make it everyone's responsibility to improve their area of the business.

The idea of managed risk is one that most people are neither familiar with nor comfortable with, so clear guidance and process are key to making it a reality. We explored process review meetings earlier in this Part, and the idea of regularly reviewing and questioning how we do things can lead to the more entrepreneurial approach that we need. However, simply giving people the opportunity to come up with ideas does not mean that we have sufficient capability to implement these ideas.

In order to easily implement new ideas and run experiments to see how something might work, we need to make sure we have considered a range of challenges. Of all the organizations interviewed for this book, there was no single solution for building an effective culture of innovation, but rather a range of techniques used in combination, which we outline here.

Market insights

One of the starting points for new initiatives and ideas for experimentation is to get great market insights. A huge array of tools is available to help us, but one very rich seam of ideas and insights is effectively used social media listening tools. We have explored these tools in Chapter 17 on process, when we looked at social media crisis management. The key to using these tools to build insights that are useful for generating new ideas is to be monitoring in a way that is both targeted enough to be focused but also broad enough to gain insights that we could not necessarily predict.

The key to achieving good monitoring is the range of words and phrases that you mention. Rather than just monitoring a limited set of words, more advanced tools have query languages that allow us to monitor certain phrases, words that are near other words, exclude phrases and carry out a host of other actions to build sets of content to analyse. The tools then allow us to easily analyse the content we have found. Again, the more advanced tools will automatically flag up topics that are changing in statistically significant ways, such as a topic that is suddenly being discussed by a number of people. We walk through an example of building a query in Chapter 17, Process and governance. Let's take this a stage further and look at a different example, and explore trends in an entire industry that can give us strategic insights for future planning.

Social monitoring tools

Although there is a wide range of social media monitoring tools available, we highly recommend the excellent Brandwatch tool. Owing to its wide range of information sources (over 90 million!), multi-language support and great sentiment analysis, it is well suited to building strategic insights. All of the social insights examples in this book were built using the tool.

SOCIAL INSIGHTS CASE STUDY   Competitor analysis for grocery delivery services – UK versus US

By setting up a query within our social media listening tool, we can monitor what brands are being mentioned within any particular area of business, as well as look at issues like the sentiment towards those brands. These insights can help shape our strategy and focus going forward. Let's explore the grocery delivery services markets in the United States and United Kingdom.

Mentions of online grocery shopping have roughly doubled since the beginning of the year in the US market, reflecting the fast changes in the market (Figure 21.1). Big retailers like Costco and Target are entering the market by partnering with start-ups like Instacart, to try to give Amazon and Google a run for their money (themselves relatively new entrants).

Figure 21.1 Mentions of grocery delivery service, UK versus US

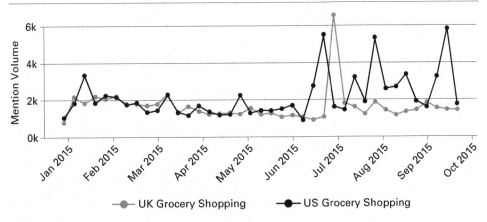

US grocery delivery services

Same-day grocery delivery is growing quickly in the United States, and although Amazon Fresh was initially the market leader, it is seeing its market share being evaporated by new entrants. These new entrants are becoming further competitive by partnering with huge established brands. Big players like Costco and Target are partnering with start-ups like Instacart, and are challenging brands like Amazon and Google in a way that would have been seen as very difficult just 12 months ago (Figure 21.2).

Figure 21.2 US grocery delivery service by volume of mentions

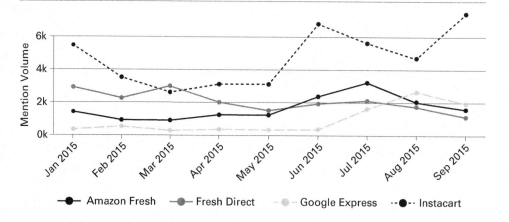

Sentiment for US grocery delivery services

Amazon Fresh is also struggling in terms of sentiment as it has a slightly lower sentiment score than most other US same-day grocery retailers. It has 63 per cent positive sentiment, while the others are all above 70 per cent currently. However, as we can see from more established markets like the United Kingdom, as market share grows and scale increases, it can be hard to maintain positive sentiment (Figure 21.3).

Sentiment for UK grocery delivery services

Grocery delivery is more established in the United Kingdom and this has allowed more time for brand sentiment to cause issues. Sentiment for UK grocery delivery services is a real issue, in part due to these brands not being purely focused on online and having large challenges in terms of logistics. US services have been able to select limited geographic areas and limited product ranges. Their UK counterparts were stuck with huge product ranges and national delivery from the outset. Asda performs worst, with only 46 per cent positive sentiment. Sainsbury's

Figure 21.3 Sentiment for US grocery delivery services

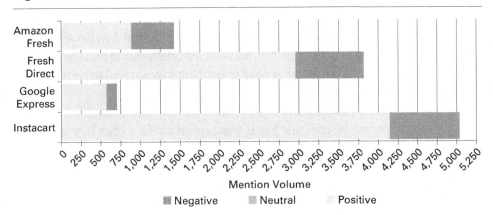

and Tesco are almost neck and neck with 58 per cent and 59 per cent positive respectively, but it should be noted that Tesco has a significantly higher market share and far higher levels of engagement online than Sainsbury's. Ocado currently has the highest level of positive sentiment (Figure 21.4).

With only around a 6–7 per cent gap between the main players, and Tesco being in the middle of a brand refocus, the market could change very quickly. The opportunity will be for established supermarkets to focus on positive customer sentiment and to grow word-of-mouth recommendations and market share.

Amazon has a chance to poach those unhappy customers from the established retailers and is focusing its efforts on growing its market share. However, its current product range does not envy those of the major established retailers and does not have the current geographic reach outside of London.

Figure 21.4 Sentiment for UK grocery delivery services

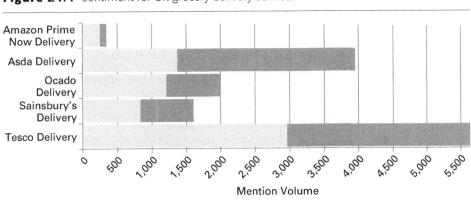

Case study conclusions

As the US market has demonstrated, pure online players can disrupt the market very quickly and even steal market share from the likes of Amazon and Google who seemed to be getting traction. However, the profitability of these new players will come into focus once they need to establish truly national delivery services and expanded product ranges.

The clear battleground is in customer sentiment, and a focus on customer service, perfect logistics and social engagement will be a key challenge for the market.

We can see from this simple case study, that insights tools can give us a great deal of insight that we can use for future planning.

Ability to experiment

Once we have an idea for trying something new (from the insights we have gleaned) or we have an existing process that we wish to attempt to improve, we need the ability to implement an experiment. The key to encouraging experimentation is having a set of processes in place to make this easy. This should include:

- regular process review and iteration suggestion process;
- regular insights review and new suggestion process;
- standard documentation/process for submitting ideas for experiment that includes objectives, measures for success, resources required and timings;
- simple agreed sign-off process with agreed turnaround time;
- pre-agreed percentage of time to be available for experimentation;
- pre-agreed budget to be available for experimentation;
- agreed service level agreements for turnaround of requests between departments;
- reward and recognition for successful experimentation;
- learning review process for all successful and unsuccessful experiments;
- clear documentation process for all findings.

Measurement frameworks

For ease of benchmarking our current level of success, as well as the ability to measure the success of any experimentation we carry out, we need to have measurement frameworks in place. Chapter 20 on measurement covers this in detail. It is worth considering, though, that a truly effective measurement framework will also normally have some technology dependencies. For example, measuring the impact of your new marketing tactic on sales leads will need your marketing channels to be connected to your Customer Relationship Management system. For this reason, achieving a Single Customer View (SCV), where our sources of data are joined up, is a clear ideal for easy testing. Realistically, achieving a true SCV is something that takes time, we need to take a realistic view and join up those systems we can on a case-by-case basis, as time and resource allow. You can review Chapter 16, Technology, for more detail on the challenges for achieving SCV.

Leadership commitment to asking challenging questions

So far we have explored two key ways of trying new ideas. The first, of reviewing our own processes, leads to innovation and improvement in current methods. The second, using insights to inform new ideas, can help expand our thinking and introduce new ideas and highlight new challenges. Neither of these methodologies always identify the potential for market disruption. We need to constantly ask ourselves what it is that could radically change our industry. As we explored in the introductory chapters of this book, there is generally a natural resistance to things that will radically change the status quo. For this reason, rather than letting our industry or business be disrupted, we must commit to disrupting ourselves. This concept may sound counter-intuitive at first: after all why would we want to change things if they are going well? However, what we really need to consider is that if something could be done radically differently to improve things, shouldn't it be us trying it, rather than one of our competitors (or more likely a brand new competitor we hadn't even considered)?

Leadership commitment to asking difficult questions is essential to keeping this focus on possible market disruption. Why do we do what we do? Why do we do it this way? What else could we be doing? What could dramatically change our market? Are we in the best position to understand the changes happening around us? The list of questions goes on, but leadership should take responsibility for trying to make sure that we maximize our potential, as well as minimizing the risk of us being blindsided.

Conclusions

The process of innovation and entrepreneurial business very often conjures up images of moments of genius or lone business people coming up with brand new ideas. In reality, we can develop a culture of innovation throughout our organizations using a set of processes and techniques. The reality is that in order to survive and flourish, we must have a culture of innovation, and we must enable our teams to act in an entrepreneurial way.

Tapping into the brave new mobile frontier

Perspectives: Innovation and disruption
Industry: Automotive
Expert: Ciaran Rogers, Host of the Digital Marketing Podcast

'Driverless cars will soon be a reality. With Google, Apple and a host of large car manufacturers all joining the development race to have the first fully automated vehicle available to buy by 2020 or sooner. But is society and the car manufacturing industry really ready for them and the complete overhaul of the automotive industry they will inevitably bring?

'It won't just be a revolution in how the car drives and navigates. That's the obvious change. It's the interesting knock-on effects in what consumers will demand from their cars once the car can drive itself that are fascinating. Think about it... If the car no longer needs a driver, then one of the core requirements cars for the last 110 years have been designed around just changed. There won't be a requirement to design around the driver needing to see from all angles and needing to be in control at all times. There is no requirement to ensure the driver is free from distraction with their eyes upon the road. In fact for passengers (and everyone in these vehicles will be passengers) the interesting revolution will occur around what those passengers choose to rest their eyes and ears upon.

'Time is a key factor here (or rather the lack of it). In the UK on average we typically spend an estimated 10 hours a week driving (Department for Transport, 2015). That's largely dead time for the driver and little better for passengers in terms of what you can do productively during transit. Based around current standard car designs, self-driving cars would simply boost our opportunity to watch the world go by. Fine for short journeys in picturesque surroundings but seriously for most car journeys? In-car entertainment is going to be key, and that will require a great deal of creativity and imagination from car manufacturers because in-car entertainment is likely to be the key feature that differentiates the must have driverless vehicle from all the other driverless drones in the market.

'To date much of the tech on offer relies on use of mobile phones or tablets within the car space but, given that the layout of a driverless vehicle can be what you want it to be, larger shared screens that offer a more immersive experience and don't have to be self-powered are a real option.

'Driverless cars have the potential to further extend what the mobile phone and standard living room tech offers consumers today. An extension of our real world and online self, but with a way better battery life and an amazingly immersive screen! With other technological shifts currently taking place it is entirely possible that Virtual Reality and Augmented Reality will all play their part in the active re-visualization of the 10 hours a week of clear space that will potentially open up for those who inhabit these autonomous vehicles. And perhaps it is this frontier of untapped time that has all the tech giants of the world scrabbling to enter into the automobile arena.

'Tech giants such as Google and Apple fully understand how hard it is to reach large audiences in a distraction-free environment. They have built complex ecosystems to hook users into their channels and in doing so are reaping big rewards from ad and product-related revenues. It makes you wonder if the car manufacturers really appreciate the true value of the time frontier they are about to open up. What is the true value of millions of people's time and attention for 7–8 hours a week? Google and Apple will be well aware. Volvo, Ford and Toyota? I'm not so sure. It isn't their business... Yet. They make cars, right? Well they did, but in less than five years they have the opportunity to be in command of one of the gateways to this untapped time frontier if Apple and Google don't steal the markets right from under their retro styled bonnets.

▶

'The car OS that powers the autonomous vehicle and its digital communications and entertainment systems has the potential to net regular ongoing monthly income throughout the life of the car, and the manufacturers are the gate-keepers to their whole market. Forget Android versus Apple IOS updates, Car OS updates and upgrades could soon become the tech industry's most talked about summer and winter releases. Top that with your car's mobile internet connectivity and you have a whole new category of options and sales to explore. Music Streaming, video streaming, voice and video calling solutions are all there to be chosen, partnered with and packaged. It's game-changing and mind-boggling when you start to think of it, and as none of these cars are actually in production yet, there is still all to play for the manufacturers who embrace the golden opportunities this new trend will open.'

Financial impact 22

To both go through any digital transformation successfully and to implement an ongoing effective digital culture we need to be able to answer one financial question. That is, can we connect what we measure elsewhere with our financial results? This ability to connect our tactical measures with our financial outcomes is essential for us to be able to quickly judge our efforts in testing out new tools and techniques. It is also essential for us to know how much of what we are doing is actually having an impact so we can iterate or change our approach. This financial measurement approach means that all our activities, from sales, marketing, HR or anywhere else, should be able to be connected in turn to our financial performance.

Financial measurement to drive change

What happens if we cannot measure the financial outcomes of a particular activity because we lack the appropriate process or, more likely, we lack the appropriate technology and systems? I have seen many organizations struggle during a digital transformation process because they cannot measure the financial impact of a particular activity or process, so find it hard to make a change. This leads to a classic case of decision paralysis. We cannot easily measure the financial outcomes of our activities, so knowing where to start is impossible. Those organizations that have succeeded in going through the digital transformation process and have established an effective digital culture have taken a clear approach to this problem. Measurement is essential, and therefore, if we cannot measure something effectively because of systems and technology, that is a very good place to start. Implementing the technology needed, or at least interim solutions, that allow us to make the connections between our activity and our end outcomes is essential. Without this connection we cannot benchmark current performance and we cannot tell if the changes we have made, had a direct impact on our end results. We are basically operating blind. A lack of being able to connect activity to financial outcomes is not an excuse for inactivity, but rather clear guidance on where we need to start part of our transformation journey.

The perfect financial measurement model

Let's be clear: there is no one single perfect solution to connecting activity to financial measurement. This is because every organization is different and therefore the subtleties of how our systems and processes will fit together will also be different. However, there is a general approach that can frame the challenge we are facing and guide us through the key steps involved.

We outlined a model for measuring digital marketing and sales activity in Chapter 20, Measurement, and this included a section on how this measurement can be connected back to financial results. This involved identifying primary objectives (in Chapter 20 this referred to web outcomes such as lead generation through a form being filled in), and we then looked at how these primary objectives could be connected to financial outcomes, either by using technology (Customer Relationship Management systems in the example given in Chapter 20) or by using sample surveying to try to tease out the connections. This principle of measuring primary objectives and then finding ways of connecting them back to financial outcomes, generally by using technology, is a solid principle that can be easily applied to digital marketing, but what about other activities like sales, HR, IT and procurement?

In fact, we can apply a similar principle and identify the primary measures, the key things that we are trying to achieve (such as the percentage of open positions that have been recruited or retaining a given percentage of staff) and estimate their impact on our financial results. Generally speaking, things like the lack of ability to recruit or retain staff will have a negative impact on other areas of the business, so these are essential areas to focus on to truly understand our financial results.

Adding non-direct activities to our measurement framework

Once we have decided upon appropriate measures for the primary objectives of each area of business, we then add these to an adapted version of our earlier defined measurement framework (see Chapter 20 for more detail). Although we may not be able to measure the direct impact of these primary objectives on financial outcomes, we can certainly estimate their current level of effectiveness and efficiency. We can also identify key indicators that will impact our ability to drive these primary objectives. Let's consider an example to explain this (Figure 22.1).

Figure 22.1 Adapting the measurement framework to look at activities that do not directly impact financial results

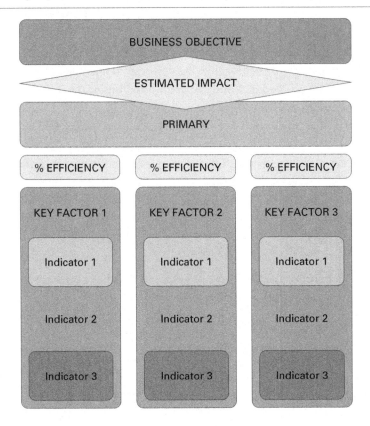

Let's start by defining the key headings here and look at what they mean:

Business objectives – our financial outcomes and business results

Estimated impact – a percentage or score that indicates how impactful we believe this primary is on our ability to achieve our financial outcomes

Primary – the key measure of the thing we are trying to achieve

Efficiency – the percentage efficiency and effectiveness we think we are currently operating at, which must be decided upon by people across the organization, not just those on the team involved

Key factors – the things we can measure that can impact our ability to achieve our primary objectives

Indicators – each of the things that we can measure and potentially change to improve our key factors

Let's now apply this to an example primary objective: that of retaining staff (Figure 22.2).

Business objectives – our financial outcomes and business results remain the same throughout each area of the business we are accessing.

Estimated impact – a score that indicates how important we think that staff retention currently is for achieving our desired financial outcomes. This should be regularly updated and indicates how important this is currently, not how efficient or effective we are at it.

Primary – in this case this is our staff retention percentage month on month.

Efficiency – the percentage efficiency and effectiveness we think we are currently operating at. These must be decided upon by people across the organization, not just those on the team involved.

Figure 22.2 Looking at the adapted measurement framework for HR and staff retention

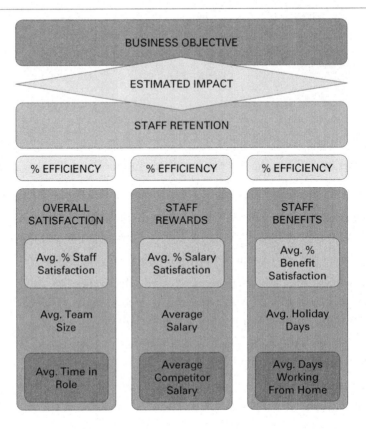

Key factors – these are the key things we can measure that we believe are impacting our ability to retain staff. In this case we have highlighted overall staff satisfaction and then staff satisfaction with two particular areas of their roles, their benefits and direct rewards. We could have any number of key factors here, each with their own indicators.

Indicators – for each of our key factors we have identified the things we can measure and potentially change to improve our key factors.

By adopting this financial results-focused approach, not just for areas like sales and marketing, but also for every other element of the business, we can make sure we do not ignore opportunities for improvement. We will also make sure we have visibility on areas of the business that could be holding back the financial performance elsewhere in the business.

Organizations without financial-based outcomes

For some organizations, the end objective is not profit, or financial contributions towards a good cause. (Just to clarify, we are not referring to charities here, as charities raise money to achieve their desired outcomes. However, if a charity is committed to changing people's attitudes, we may need to consider the approach outlined here.) It may be that your desired outcome is a change in attitude or lifestyle. For example, an anti-obesity charity may aim to change people's behaviour around diet and exercise. Alternatively, a lobbying organization may aim to change government policy on a particular cause. In both cases we cannot measure our return directly in terms of financial outcomes. In both cases, however, it is useful to consider using the approach of 'financial equivalents'. In the case of the obesity charity we may consider what the medical cost would likely be to treat a person if his or her obesity were not managed. For the lobbying organization, we could consider what the equivalent cost would be without the change in government law or approach. Although neither of these 'equivalent cost' approaches factor in the human element of the equation, such as the improvement in somebody's happiness due to being more physically active, or the distress prevented by changing a government policy, they are both approaches that can help us to argue the value of the approach we are taking. By removing any subjective element of the argument and focusing purely on financial equivalents, we make it easier to debate and justify our required resources.

Conclusions

Implementing measurement frameworks that allow us to make the connection between our areas of activity and our financial performance is essential to building an effective digital culture. The connection allows for easy, and importantly quick, decision-making about where to spend our efforts and resources. Not only do we need this financial focus during the process of transformation, but it is essential to keep our organizations focused as we continue to adapt to the changing world around us.

Measurement framework template and example

For a full template that you can adapt, along with example data for a wide area of different business departments visit the online resources that accompany this book:

www.targetinternet.com/digitalculture

PART FOUR
Keeping up with change

Keeping measurement at the core

Throughout the digital culture framework we looked at the various aspects of going through a digital transformation process, but it is important to remember that the process is different in every organization. You will not actually fully map out the process until it is underway, and you will most likely need to change your plans along the way. What is essential, however, is that we end up with a set of techniques and processes that allow us to keep iterating.

The risk of digital transformation is that we go through the process, fix various issues, such as technology integration and measurement frameworks, and then think that we have completed the process. The reason this book is focused on building digital culture, not just about digital transformation, is that the change required will never stop. Building a digital culture means that as well as fixing things like technology integration, we also put in place processes and approaches that allow us to constantly adapt and improve. Digital transformation with no ongoing plan means you are likely to be back where you started given some time. The environment around you will change, your systems and processes will get out of date, new channels will arrive that you have no approach to testing and suddenly you are struggling again.

An effective digital culture gives us the range of techniques and tools we need to be prepared for constant change. The key to this culture is keeping measurement at the heart of everything, but not in a way that adds a burden to measure constantly. What this means in practice is a series of techniques that put measurement and iterative improvement on autopilot.

We have covered these steps in The Digital Culture Framework, but it is worth highlighting the key techniques we need in place for an effective ongoing approach to improvement.

1. Commitment and agility to experiment

The concept of constant experimentation should be embraced throughout the organization. Not only do we need to build review processes that make us automatically review how we approach everything we do, we also need to make the experimentation itself as easy as possible. This means building agility into the organization with things like pre-agreed internal service level agreements for turnaround times and simplified sign-off processes.

2. Measurement frameworks

Effective measurement frameworks that allow us to easily connect our tactical activity to our financial performance mean we can see the results of our experimentation quickly and easily. The measurement frameworks outlined in the measurement and financial sections of this book are designed to allow us to focus on the tactical elements of our efforts that may have an impact on our desired business objectives. This focus on ROI leads to much simpler internal communication and simplified sign-off of new initiatives (due to easier justification of any new approaches).

3. Single Customer View

Well-integrated technology that allows us to fully understand our customers (and potential customers) across multiple channels is essential so that we can personalize our approach to cut through the noisy environment we operate in. Customers expect higher levels of service and personalization, and this trend will only increase as time goes on. A Single Customer View gives us the opportunity to interrogate and utilize a range of data sources in an integrated way.

4. Process review

Ongoing process review is part of out commitment to ongoing iteration and improvement. The review process is a way of putting iterative improvement on auto-drive, but this needs to be accompanied by a culture of challenging ourselves and our working practices.

5. Ongoing skills development

All staff must be committed to constantly developing their own skills, and the organization needs to provide both the environment and the tools to help everyone to continue on this journey. Blended learning solutions should be available to expand skills and track progress and gamification-based approaches can have a significant impact on uptake.

6. Broad insights

Iteration of existing approaches is great, but we also need sufficient stimuli to make sure we are considering issues and challenges beyond our day-to-day horizon. Insights tools and the processes used to review these tools are essential to creating a culture of innovation.

7. Leadership

All the tools and techniques available will achieve little without clear direction from senior leaders on their importance. We also need senior leaders to constantly ask difficult questions about our organizations and keep an eye out for ways in which we may radically change our approach. In order to avoid market disruption, we must be constantly looking to disrupt our own markets and organizations.

Guaranteed prediction

This is the slowest pace of change you will see going forward.

Conclusions

Measurement should not be limited to reporting. A measurement-based approach allows for constant review and iteration. This commitment to iteration is at the heart of an effective digital culture that helps us thrive in a constantly changing environment.

Separating the ephemeral from the enduring 24

One of the most commonly asked questions, particularly when dealing with things like new social media channels, is 'Is this important and will it last?'. The truth of the situation is that we have very little idea something is important until it finally is, and it is therefore near on impossible to answer this question. There are, however, a range of approaches we can take that mean we are likely to have a clear view on a social channel's (or anything else) current state of relevance and importance.

Let's look at an example. Many people dismissed Twitter in its early years. They logged in, didn't understand it and therefore didn't see the value. However, the platform grew in popularity, its functionality grew and it became an essential social network for many organizations. Those who stuck with their initial impressions continued to dismiss it, and missed out on an important opportunity to engage with their audience, drive traffic to their websites and gain market insights. So how do we avoid these kinds of judgements that lead to lost opportunity? Equally, what happens if we invest heavily in a channel that fails?

Experimentation is key

Throughout this book we have demonstrated that the adoption of constant experimentation in every aspect of our workplace is essential for a fast-changing environment. This equally applies when we are unsure of the outcome. If we continue with the example of a new social channel, we are able to make relatively low-risk experiments early on when audiences are still relatively low. Although we may not get huge levels of positive ROI, we will have gained insights into the channel and be able to see if it holds promise. In reality though, if we have pre-committed certain time or financial resources to experimentation, we can quickly know if we have suitable resources to commit to test the channel properly. There is little point in an experiment that is under-resourced. All this will do is glean no positive outcomes and skew our view of the channel going forward.

The risk of not continuing

Very often we test something, have little success, so decide it was down to the channel (for example). However, a real commitment to experimentation means that we know that there is a wide range of variables involved in any experiment, and until we have exhausted all possibilities for these variables, we don't have a full understanding. For example, if I use Twitter and I get no response it could be a wide range of factors. My content could have been unsuitable for my audience. The time of day I tweeted could have been a poor choice. My tone of voice might have been wrong. I might not have built enough of an audience to get any traction and may need to use paid placement. Until I have exhausted these possibilities then I don't know if my experiment is a success or not. Happily I don't need to start every experiment with no idea what will work and exhaust every possible combination of factors. There is enough guidance on best practice that I should be able to start from a fairly strong position in the first place.

But what happens if we do a thorough test and find a channel simply does not work for us? Will it look bad if we pull out of the channel? There is a fairly simple answer to this question. If you believe that enough people whose opinions you care about are watching you on this channel, then how is the experiment a failure in the first place? And if not, it will not damage your reputation to remove yourself from a channel. So the key is only go in if you are resourced to test properly, and then make sure you do test properly.

Insights review and external opinion

It is easy to not see the relevance of things we do not fully understand, or to be blinkered by our current focus. For this reason, it is essential to get good external insights. These can come from insights tools, external consultants' industry conferences and any other number of information sources (and we should never be limited to a single source). Trying to put a value against the time and resources needed to attend industry events, listen to webinars, etc, can be challenging, but the risk of not attending, at least a carefully selected percentage, offers a much greater risk. A process orientated approach can again minimize the amount of decision-making and sign-offs that are required. We can assign predefined time and resources to insights-gathering as part of our approach to training and upskilling.

Conclusions

There is no magic bullet to identifying what is and is not important in a fast-changing environment, but we can organize processes and techniques that give us the best opportunity to be well informed. We can also build a culture of experimentation and iteration so we can truly trust the opinions and insights we build.

Three things to watch

Making predictions about the future of digital technology is no mean feat. After all, if it was easy, we would already have the answers, wouldn't we? The pace and disruptive nature of change means it is almost impossible to predict further than a couple of years, and undoubtedly anything we write in this book could be out of date by the time it is published.

That said, there are a few big developments we think it is worth spotlighting in this 'three things to watch' penultimate chapter.

Connected living

In its 2015 CEO Briefing, Accenture explained: 'Many recent technological advances have been distributed in nature, producing a world where existing objects – from industrial machines to cars, refrigerators, and even people, plants or animals – can be connected to the Internet to collect and receive data. This developing frontier, known as the Internet of Things (IoT), is generating a multitude of new opportunities.' (Accenture, 2015)

This is clearly a significant subject area with many potential applications and implications, but the one we would like to focus on is connected living.

Connected living specifically looks at the role that IoT connected devices will have on consumers' lives, rather than their industrial or public sector applications. Consider a few examples:

- Your home surveillance is connected to your smartphone, with automatic alerts for movements, such as checking your kids have arrived home from school or seeing that a delivery courier has arrived.

- Your car's location is linked to your home appliances, automatically turning on lights, heating or your oven so that they are automatically ready for you when you arrive home from work.

- Your smartwatch or wearable fitness technology monitors your health and can send automatic alerts to your GP or physician if an appointment is needed to review your blood pressure or heart rate.

- Your fridge tracks your product consumption and automatically orders fresh milk, juice or vegetables from your favourite grocery retailer, or for delivery from Amazon's new grocery service.

In 2015, there were an estimated 5 billion connected devices on the planet. Estimates vary, but predictions for 2020 show a significant increase, with Gartner forecasting 21 billion connected devices in use (Gartner, 2015), and two-thirds of that growth is predicted to come from consumer devices. Twenty-one billion devices. That is more than three times today's total world population.

While consumer adoption of various different technologies is yet to play out, there is no doubt that this trend will have significant implications for organizations, beyond just the revenue potential.

First, *privacy*. Consumers are already nervous about how much Facebook, Apple and Google know about their e-mails, interactions with friends, search history and location. As machine-to-machine (M2M) connectivity increases at the rate of knots predicted by Gartner, the depth of insight into the lives of consumers will be staggering. How will technology providers, with an already chequered history when it comes to personal data, reassure customers and help them to manage their privacy in relation to their health and consumption data, for instance?

Second, *security*. Cybersecurity has been deemed a national strategic priority by governments in both the United Kingdom and the United States, not to mention the growing focus being taken by businesses. Cyberattacks, such as denial of service (DoS) attacks on banks, and hacks for personal and financial data, such as from utility and healthcare providers, are becoming increasingly common, not to mention growing concern around cyberterrorism. With the rapid predicted growth in devices over the next few years, the risks are mounting. Can governments and businesses stay ahead of (alleged) foreign state-sponsored hackers and the community of computer scientists and programmers who see breaching digital security as sport?

Third, *data*. Businesses are already struggling with the masses of data flowing into their organizations. This looks set to increase dramatically, leaving us wondering whether 'big data' was the solution it purported to be, or more of a thinly veiled warning. There are practical implications for data storage and processing, of course, but more significantly is knowing how to extract value from that data, what to listen to and what to discard.

However this progresses, it is certainly one to watch. Keep an eye on what Gartner, Cisco, McKinsey, Amazon, Apple and Google have to say in this area.

What if the uberization of talent becomes mainstream?

We are all aware of the biggest winners of collaborative consumption, or the 'sharing economy', as it is better known: Airbnb and Uber. The first revolutionized travel and holidays by enabling property owners to rent out rooms or whole apartments, houses and villas, supported by meaningful traveller stories (reviews) and a genuine peer-to-peer model. Uber brought the concept of the 'gig economy' to taxis, with a differentiated proposition and typically cheaper pricing.

These are two well-known success stories, both securing market valuations in the billions of dollars (around US $25 billion and US $62 billion respectively, as of 2015). But what if their model were applied to digital talent? There are already examples of what some call the 'uberization' of talent, but what if this went beyond a fringe idea and into the mainstream? Consider the current dysfunction of talent recruitment generally.

First, it is *expensive*. Agency fees range from 15 to 30 per cent (on average) and the time-cost of recruiting (once you have gone through all of the internal processes your business uses), on-boarding and waiting for people to become effective in-role. Add to that the management time involved in the recruitment process, and the potential lack of resource, and you can be forgiven for looking at that final appointment decision as something of a gamble (or mitigated risk, at least).

Second, it is *time consuming*. Few, if any, organizations have people (outside of HR, in a functional capacity) whose role is dedicated to recruitment. Of course, you may have HR support, talent acquisition professionals and other business partners to aid in the process, but you cannot completely remove the hiring manager from the equation. One of our interviewees in the research for this book gave an example of a senior manager building digital capability from scratch, having to work through more than 1,000 interviews to build a team of approximately 70 people over the period of almost a year.

Third, it is *uncertain*. Despite advances in interview techniques such as personality profiling, psychometric testing and good old-fashioned competency-based interviews, you never really know if there is a fit until you are days or even weeks into an appointment. Add to that the concept of fluid working and (if not something of a generalization) preference for project- and portfolio-based roles that the iGeneration might favour, you could be looking at a great deal of flux in your digital talent base.

But what if recruiting *some* digital talent was more like booking an Airbnb room or an Uber ride? What if you had access to a talent pool with far greater scale than regionally organized recruitment agencies? What if you could fast-track the process and benefit from more scientific matching? What if you could dispense with generic references and base your decisions on more authentic, detailed peer reviews and feedback?

What would that mean for how you think about resourcing? What time and cost savings could be on offer, not to mention the potential for a more flexible, on-demand workforce without the cost structure of agencies, consultancy or interim fees?

It may never happen. It may only take root in certain locations, sectors or disciplines. Or it could completely upend the digital talent economy. Either way, worth a watch.

Artificial intelligence

For many, artificial intelligence (AI) still feels like the talk of science-fiction enthusiasts, but the reality is, the machine learning journey has already begun. Pop culture has taught us that the quest to take machines to a level of intelligence that matches humans can only end in tragedy. The dystopian futures imagined in a world of super-smart machines all point to one conclusion: once machines match human intelligence, they will evolve beyond us and we will no longer be needed. Hal9000, iRobot, The Avengers' Ultron and Skynet's judgement day all point to an extinction-level event for humanity.

But that is not what we are suggesting you keep an eye on as you grapple with digital transformation and culture change. We are not here to debate whether the rise of the machines will spell the end of the world as we know it; the developments in machine learning are decades away from the point where machine and human intelligence will be on a par. What we are here to discuss, however, is how the present advancements in AI – which are already creeping into how we live and work – might impact businesses in the medium term.

The most commonly known example of AI in practice today, is IBM's Watson, an evolution from the famous IBM Deep Blue supercomputer that beat world chess champion Garry Kasparov in 1997.

Watson is at the forefront of IBM's cognitive computing capabilities, and it is not a distant research initiative, it already powers approximately 100 commercialized solutions. As IBM describes it, Watson 'is a technology platform that uses natural language processing and machine learning to reveal insights from large amounts of unstructured data'. Much, much faster than humans could ever do. It is a question-answering application that can sift through unimaginable quantities of data from a vast array of sources, and applies dozens of individual algorithms to understand, reason and learn, and ultimately deliver insight and answers with high levels of confidence.

Applications have largely been focused on healthcare, finance, education and medical research, but in late 2015 IBM made its first significant moves into marketing decision-making. Watson analytics can now aid with research, segmentation and media planning, as well as analysing the drivers of revenue and performance.

As the sophistication of Watson's (and others') analytical capabilities develop further through new applications and solutions, this will begin to bring powerful ways for businesses to diagnose and address problems faster than ever before. Imagine being able to feed data from CRM, sales, customer meetings, website analytics, product usage performance and more into a single system that can process and interpret it rapidly, simply by being asked questions like 'who are my most profitable customers and how do I find more like them?'.

Existential questions aside, the advances in cognitive computing that are only just starting to permeate the marketing, advertising and digital world will continue at pace and have a potentially significant disruptive effect. Without a doubt, one to watch.

Epilogue

We carried out over 200 hours of interviews and research for this book, have consulted for dozens of organizations going through the digital transformation process and have personally trained thousands of individuals in the strategic skills needed to implement effective digital culture over the years. What is fascinating is that although there is no one solution for achieving digital transformation and an effective ongoing digital culture, there are common patterns that successful organizations share.

You are going to struggle at times – practical advice

We have tried to highlight these common factors and structures throughout the book, but we think it wise to finish on some words of reassurance. In every transformation process we have witnessed and been part of, there have been times when we have struggled. Whether it was getting past the roadblock of a technology integration issue, or getting buy-in from a resistant group of the team, we have had problems that we struggled to find solutions for. The solutions almost always involved making sure we had senior leadership on board as the leaders of the project. If this was not the case, these blocks would take much longer to resolve.

The other thing that often leads to problems is trying to do too much at once. 'Boiling the ocean' syndrome happens a lot in transformation projects, and it is natural as there is often so much to do. One of the biggest challenges that cause this approach are the many dependencies between projects. For this reason we generally recommend starting with a measurement framework. Once this is established you will be able to judge the success of some elements of your activity and iterate improvement. However, in many cases, technology prevents the effective implementation of an end-to-end measurement framework. This should lead to two steps. Firstly, develop an imperfect measurement technique that is as good as you can create and roll with it. Secondly, make the technology solution that solves your measurement issues a priority. Once this is fixed, everything else becomes easier.

Things happen in fits and starts

Unless you are very lucky, are hugely resourced and you encounter no problems, digital transformation happens in fits and starts. A transformation process generally involves fixing a series of highly complicated interdependent projects. This will mean unexpected delays and periods that seem to lack progress. While it is our job to minimize these periods, don't be surprised by them. Be willing to revisit your plans and priorities constantly and change what you are focusing on, based on what is blocking your path.

The bigger the block you experience, the more people whose advice you should seek. This is best explained with an example. We were working with a global technology company and were trying to implement a new Customer Relationship Management (CRM) system that would allow us to measure more effectively and have huge impact on our ability to implement most of the rest of our plans. After weeks of delays and frustration caused by a third-party supplier, the project was losing momentum. We decided we needed some outside counsel and set up meetings with pretty much everyone we knew, who knew anything about CRM systems. Three meetings later I discovered a new version of a cloud-based CRM was about to launch that looked like a better solution, and the vendor was willing to give a huge discount to get some initial customers up and running. We cancelled the original project, started from scratch and finished ahead of our initial schedule in the end. This was only possible for two reasons. The first was involvement of outside counsel leading to new and more innovative ideas, and the second was complete buy-in from leadership and thankfully procurement. You need as many people completely brought into the journey as possible and you need to communicate regularly.

The journey never ends

It is an odd sensation that once your transformation projects end, the real work begins. That is what Digital Culture is all about. Building an environment where you can work smarter, more effectively and constantly challenge yourself and those around you. Our experience is that effective Digital

Culture leads to more fulfilling working environments, more successful organizations and happier employees. It is worth the effort – keep on going!

Good luck – we would love to hear your insights and experiences. Tweet your thoughts or give us a shout @DanielRowles, @ThinkStuff and #DigiCultureBook.

Daniel Rowles and Thomas Brown

APPENDIX: THE DIGITAL CULTURE TOOLKIT

Throughout this book we have highlighted a number of models and techniques that you can use to help with your digital transformation process. You will find a range of templates, tools and accompanying support materials including case studies, blogs, videos and podcasts.

Included in the resources:

Analysis tool to benchmark your organization's readiness and implementation level for achieving an effective digital culture.

Individual analysis tool to benchmark your digital marketing and technology skills against industry averages.

Step-by-step guide to the measurement framework laid out in the Digital Culture Framework.

Templates to help you build your own measurement frameworks.

Over 100 episodes of the Digital Marketing Podcast with audio interviews with brands like Microsoft and Adobe on their latest innovations.

www.targetinternet.com/digitalculture

REFERENCES AND FURTHER READING

Accenture [accessed 25 July 2016] CEO Briefing 2015: From Productivity to Outcomes [online] www.accenture.com/gb-en/insight-ceo-briefing-2015-productivity-outcomes

Aronowitz, S, De Smet, A and McGinty, D [accessed 25 July 2016] Getting organizational redesign right, *McKinsey Quarterly* [Online] www.mckinsey.com/business-functions/organization/our-insights/getting-organizational-redesign-right

Austin, Scott, Canipe, Chris and Slobin, Sarah [accessed 12 August 2016] The Billion Dollar Startup Club: Company Valuations, *The Wall Street Journal* [Online] http://graphics.wsj.com/billion-dollar-club/

BBC [accessed 12 August 2016] Uber joins race for driverless cars [Online] http://www.bbc.co.uk/news/business-36339340

Best, Richard [accessed 12 August 2016] Automattic – An IPO Candidate in 2016? *Investopedia* [Online] http://www.investopedia.com/articles/markets/012716/automattic-ipo-candidate-2016.asp

Bort, Julie [accessed 12 September 2016] Billion-dollar startup Automattic hires employees without ever meeting them or talking to them on the phone, *Business Insider UK* [Online] http://uk.businessinsider.com/automattic-hires-employees-automatically-2016-1

Bughin, J, Holley, A and Mellbye, A [accessed 25 July 2016] Cracking the digital code: McKinsey Global Survey results, September, *McKinsey Quarterly* [Online] www.mckinsey.com/business-functions/business-technology/our-insights/cracking-the-digital-code

CIM [accessed 12 August 2016] What is Marketing? The Chartered Institute of Marketing [Online] http://www.cim.co.uk/more/getin2marketing/what-is-marketing/

Coase, R (1937) [accessed 12 August 2016] The Nature of the Firm [Online] https://en.wikipedia.org/wiki/The_Nature_of_the_Firm

Coughlan, Sean [accessed 12 August 2016] Time spent online 'overtakes TV' among youngsters, BBC [Online] http://www.bbc.co.uk/news/education-35399658

Department for Transport (2015) [accessed 12 September 2016] National Travel Survey: England 2014 [Online] https://www.gov.uk/government/uploads/system/uploads/attachment_data/file/457752/nts2014-01.pdf

Fitzgerald, Michael [accessed 12 August 2016] The Nine Obstacles to Digital Transformation, *MIT Sloan Management Review* [Online] http://sloanreview.mit.edu/article/the-nine-obstacles-to-digital-transformation/

Friedrich, R, Péladeau, P and Mueller, K [accessed 25 July 2016] Adapt, disrupt, transform, disappear: The 2015 Chief Digital Officer Study, PwC [Online] www.strategyand.pwc.com/reports/chief-digital-officer-study

Gandel, Stephen [accessed 12 August 2016] These Are the 10 Most Valuable Companies in the Fortune 500, *Fortune* [Online] http://fortune.com/2016/02/04/most-valuable-companies-fortune-500-apple/

Gartner [accessed 25 July 2016] Gartner Says 6.4 Billion Connected "Things" Will Be in Use in 2016, Up 30 Percent From 2015 [Online] www.gartner.com/newsroom/id/3165317

Gillett, R [accessed 25 July 2016] Why Our Brains Crave Storytelling In Marketing, *Fast Company* [Online] www.fastcompany.com/3031419/hit-the-ground-running/why-our-brains-crave-storytelling-in-marketing

Iyengar, Rishi [accessed 12 August 2016] This is how long your business will last according to science, *Fortune* [Online] http://fortune.com/2015/04/02/this-is-how-long-your-business-will-last-according-to-science/

LinkedIn Talent Solutions [accessed 12 August 2016] Global Recruiting Trends 2016 [Online] https://business.linkedin.com/content/dam/business/talent-solutions/global/en_us/c/pdfs/GRT16_GlobalRecruiting_100815.pdf

MacDonald, Steven [accessed 29 July 2016] 12 Amazing CRM Charts You Don't Want To Miss, SuperOffice [Online] http://www.superoffice.com/blog/crm-charts/

Martin, Dave [accessed 12 August 2016] Automattic's remote hiring process, Dave Martin's Blog [Online] https://davemart.in/2015/04/22/inside-automattics-remote-hiring-process/

Mendelow, A (1991) 'Stakeholder Mapping', Proceedings of the 2nd International Conference on Information Systems, Cambridge, MA (Cited in Wikipedia [accessed 25 July 2016] Stakeholder analysis [Online] https://en.wikipedia.org/wiki/Stakeholder_analysis)

Microsoft [accessed 12 August 2016] Microsoft HoloLens [Online] https://www.microsoft.com/microsoft-hololens/en-us

Milligan, B [accessed 25 July 2016] Desktop banking use falls, as users switch to apps, BBC [Online] www.bbc.co.uk/news/business-36857433

Moore, Nicholas [accessed 12 August 2016] Top Marketing Statistics for 2016, Experian [Online] http://www.experian.co.uk/blogs/latest-thinking/top-marketing-statistics-2015/

Mosbergen, D [accessed 25 July 2016] French Legislation Suggests Employees Deserve The Right To Disconnect, *Huffington Post* [Online] www.huffingtonpost.com/entry/work-emails-france-labor-law_us_57455130e4b03ede4413515a

Negroponte, N [accessed 25 July 2016] Beyond Digital, *Wired* [Online] www.wired.com/1998/12/negroponte-55/

Seetharaman, Deepa [accessed 12 August 2016] Facebook Revenue Soars on Ad Growth, *The Wall Street Journal* [Online] http://www.wsj.com/articles/facebook-revenue-soars-on-ad-growth-1461787856

Statista [accessed 9 September 2016] Number of 1st level connections of LinkedIn users as of March 2016 [Online] www.statista.com/statistics/264097/number-of-1st-level-connections-of-linkedin-users/

Tech City [accessed 12 July 2016] 'Tech Nation 2016: Transforming UK Industries' [Online] https://www.swipe.to/9057ct

Treanor, J [accessed 25 July 2016] Digital revolution presents banks with more change in 10 years than last 200, *The Guardian* [Online] www.theguardian.com/business/2014/oct/26/banks-digital-revolution-change-regulation-job-losses

Web Technology Surveys [accessed 12 August 2016] Usage statistics and market share of Google Analytics for websites, W³Techs [Online] https://w3techs.com/technologies/details/ta-googleanalytics/all/all

Wordpress [accessed 12 August 2016] Wordpress: About Us [Online] https://wordpress.com/about/

INDEX

Note: *Italics* indicate a Figure or Table.

CPSIA information can be obtained
at www.ICGtesting.com
Printed in the USA
LVOW13s0130011217
558158LV00019B/264/P